Contents

A GRAMMAR BRUSH-UP

The Basics

Parts of Speech

BARRON'S FOREIGN LANGUAGE GUIDES

Master
the Basics

JAPANESE

SECOND EDITION

Nobuo Akiyama
Professorial Lecturer, Japanese Language
The Paul H. Nitze
School of Advanced International Studies
The Johns Hopkins University
and
Carol Akiyama
Language Training Consultant
Washington, D.C.

BARRON'S

We thank Dimitry Popow, our editor, for his invaluable and unfailing help.

All inquiries should be addressed to:
Barron's Educational Series, Inc.
250 Wireless Boulevard
Hauppauge, New York 11788
www.barronseduc.com

Library of Congress Control Number: 2008929993

ISBN-13: 978-0-7641-3971-0
ISBN-10: 0-7641-3971-1

Printed in Canada

9 8 7 6 5 4 3 2 1

Special Topics

Preface

This book is one of a series of grammar reference guides. Designed for students of Japanese and others who want to improve their knowledge of Japanese grammar, it enables you to determine how much you already know, helps to reinforce your skills, and increases your knowledge of this language.

Whether you are just beginning your study of Japanese or have had some basic courses and want to refresh your memory, this book is for you. Previous knowledge has not been taken for granted; definitions and explanations are simple and concise, and examples use and reuse a core of basic vocabulary.

The book is divided into three sections: The Basics, Parts of Speech, and Special Topics.

- In the Basics section you will find a nontechnical and easy-to-follow discussion of Japanese sounds, spelling conventions, and word-order patterns.
- The Parts of Speech section consists of the nouns, pronouns, particles, verbs, adjectives, and adverbs that make up the Japanese language.
- The Special Topics section comprises numbers, expressions for telling time, language for family relationships, useful words and phrases, and more.

To find out how to use this book, just read ahead!

How to Use This Book

In the chapters that follow, a numerical decimal system has been used with the symbol § in front of it. This was done so that you may find quickly and easily the reference to a particular point in basic Japanese grammar when you use the index. For example, if you look up the entry "particles" in the index, you will find the reference given as §6. Sometimes additional § reference numbers are given when the entry you consulted is mentioned in other areas in the chapter §.

First take the diagnostic test at the beginning of the book. Check the answers provided at the end of the test and grade yourself. Be sure to look at the summary that relates the questions to the chapters in the book. This process will help you to see those areas in which you are strong and those that need more study.

Next go through the main part of the book, the "Grammar Brush-Up," at your own pace. You might choose to start with the sections that the diagnostic test showed were your weakest. Or you might prefer to start at the beginning and go to the end, spending as little or as much time as you need on each section.

Finally, turn to the "Let's Review" section at the end, and do the exercises—250 questions and activities with answers keyed to the numerical reference system in the "Grammar Brush-Up." The results will show you how far you've come in your study of Japanese!

FIND OUT WHAT YOU KNOW

Test Yourself

THE BASICS

Circle the letter for each correct answer below.

1. The pronunciation of Japanese vowels is similar to that of
   A. English   B. French   C. Italian   D. Spanish

2. The Japanese vowel *e* is pronounced like the vowel sound in the English word
   A. Pete   B. pet   C. been   D. lean

3. In Japanese, the vowels, $\bar{a}$, *ei*, *ii*, $\bar{o}$, and $\bar{u}$ should be
   A. lengthened   B. shortened   C. omitted
   D. whispered

4. The Japanese consonant *s* is never pronouned like the *s* in the following English word
   A. so   B. ask   C. reason   D. messy

5. A doubled consonant in a Japanese word means you should
   A. repeat the sound twice
   B. hold the sound longer

6. The commonly used expression for the romanization of Japanese words is
   A. hiragana   B. romaji   C. katakana   D. kanji

7. In a typical Japanese sentence the verb is found at the
   A. beginning   B. middle   C. end

PARTS OF SPEECH

Write the Japanese for each of the following:

8. book _____ books _____

9. Mr. Morita _____ Mrs. Abe _____

10. name (polite form) _____

11. English teacher _____

3

Complete the sentences below by writing the Japanese pronoun.

12. Kinō _____ ga kimashita. (he)

13. Meri san wa _____ o shitte imasu. (me)

14. _____ kimashita. (someone)

15. _____ de shinasai. (yourself)

Fill in the Japanese particle for each sentence below.

16. Tegami _____ kimashita. (subject marker)

17. Sono hon _____ yomimashita. (direct object marker)

18. Watakushi _____ uchi wa koko desu.
    (possessive marker)

19. Horiguchi san wa, kirei desu _____ . (question marker)

Fill in the correct verb form (polite) in the sentences below.

20. Kore wa, hon _____ . (is)

21. Koko ni kōen ga _____ . (was)

22. Watakushi wa, kōhi o _____ . (don't drink)

23. Tegami o _____ . (am writing)

24. Ginza ni _____ . (let's go)

Circle the letter for the meaning of each item below.

25. chiisai kuruma
    A. young crew   B. small car   C. delicious cheese
    D. big top

26. shinsetsuna sensei
    A. kind teacher   B. bad driver   C. quiet room
    D. healthy person

27. ōkiino
    A. big   B. bigger   C. biggest   D. big one

Fill in the correct adverb in the sentences below.

28. Gakkō wa, _____ ni arimasu. (here)

29. _____ shinbun o yomimasu. (every day)

30. _____ shimashō. (again)

SPECIAL TOPICS

Check the box that corrresponds to the figures for the Japanese number.

31. roku

    5   ☐

    6   ☐

    8   ☐

32. hachijūichi

    41   ☐

    63   ☐

    81   ☐

33. nanasen

    7,000   ☐

    8,000   ☐

    9,000   ☐

Write the following times of day in Japanese.

34. It's 5 o'clock.   _____

35. It's 5:30.   _____

36. It's 5:45.   _____

Circle the letter of the correct classifier.

37. one person
    A. hitori   B. ippon   C. ichimai

38. two books
    A. futari   B. nihon   C. nisatsu

39. three bottles
    A. sanbon   B. sansatsu   C. sanmai

Fill in the blanks with the Japanese in the following
sentences.

40. Kyō wa, _____ desu. (Tuesday)

41. _____ benkyō shimashita. (this morning)

42. _____ Tōkyō ni ikimasu. (every day)

Match the words in the left column with their meaning in the
right column.

43. the first (of the month)   A. ichinichi

44. one day   B. tsuitachi

45. one month   C. ikkagetsu

Write the appropriate Japanese below.

46. _____ desu. (winter)

47. _____ wa dō desu ka. (weather)

48. _____ desu. (cold)

Find the word for the family member in the right column to
match the Japanese word in the left column.

49. okusan   A. cousin

50. okāsan   B. wife

51. itoko   C. mother

Complete the useful expressions below by supplying the missing Japanese.

52. Ohayō _____ . (Good morning.)

53. _____ , kekkō desu. (No, thank you.)

54. _____ ga, wakarimasu ka. (Do you understand English?)

55. Mō _____ onegai shimasu. (Could you repeat it, please?)

56. Onaka ga, _____ imasu. (I'm hungry.)

For each Japanese word borrowed from English, choose the meaning.

57. batā
    A. batter   B. barter   C. butter   D. but

58. sūpā
    A. super   B. superb   C. spa
    D. supermarket

59. manshon
    A. house   B. condominium   C. mansion
    D. apartment

60. wanpīsu
    A. dress   B. war and peace   C. one piece
    D. one pea soup

Answers

1. D.   Spanish

2. B.   pet

3. A.   lengthened

4. C.   reason

5. B.   hold the sound longer

6. B.   romaji

7. C.   end

8. hon; hon

9. Morita san; Abe san

10. onamae

11. eigo no sensei

12. kare

13. watakushi

14. Dareka

15. Jibun

16. ga

17. o

18. no

19. ka

20. desu

21. arimashita

22. nomimasen

23. kaite imasu

24. ikimashō

25. B. small car

26. A. kind teacher

27. D. big one

28. koko

29. Mainichi

30. Mata

31. 6

32. 81

33. 7,000

34. Goji desu.

35. Goji han desu.

36. Goji yonjūgofun desu; Rokuji jūgofun mae desu.

37. A. hitori

38. C. nisatsu

39. A. sanbon

40. kayōbi

41. Kesa

42. Mainichi

43. B. tsuitachi

44. A. ichinichi

45. C. ikkagetsu

46. Fuyu

47. Tenki

48. Samui

49. B. wife

50. C.   mother

51. A.   cousin

52. gozaimasu

53. lie

54. Eigo

55. ichido

56. suite

57. C.   butter

58. D.   supermarket

59. B.   condominium

60. A.   dress

Diagnostic Analysis

Section	Question Numbers	Number of Answers	
		Right	Wrong
THE BASICS			
1. Pronunciation	1, 2, 3, 4, 5		
2. The Japanese Writing System	6		
3. Word Order	7		
PARTS OF SPEECH			
4. Nouns	8, 9, 10, 11		
5. Pronouns	12, 13, 14, 15		
6. Particles	16, 17, 18, 19		
7. Verbs	20, 21, 22, 23, 24		
8. Adjectives	25, 26, 27		
9. Adverbs	28, 29, 30		
SPECIAL TOPICS			
10. Numbers	31, 32, 33		
11. Telling Time	34, 35, 36		
12. Classifiers	37, 38, 39		
13. Days, Months, Seasons, Weather	40, 41, 42, 43, 44, 45, 46, 47, 48		
14. Family	49, 50, 51		
15. Useful Words and Phrases	52, 53, 54, 55, 56, 57, 58, 59, 60		
TOTAL QUESTIONS:	60		

Use the following scale to see how you did.

57 to 60 right	Excellent
53 to 56 right	Very Good
49 to 52 right	Average
45 to 48 right	Below Average
Fewer than 45 right	Unsatisfactory

A GRAMMAR BRUSH-UP

The Basics

Pronuncation Guide

**§1.1
WHAT ARE
VOWELS AND
CONSONANTS?**

There are two kinds of sounds in any language.

- *Vowels* are produced by air passing out through the mouth without being blocked. The letters that represent these sounds are **a, e, i, o, u**.

- *Consonants*, on the other hand, are produced by blockage (partial or complete) of the air. The remaining alphabet letters are used to represent consonant sounds: **b, c, d**, etc.

Japanese isn't difficult to pronounce if you follow a few simple guidelines. Take the time to read this section, and try out each sound presented.

**§1.2
VOWELS**

If you have studied Spanish, it may help you to know that Japanese vowels are more like those of Spanish than English.

The following vowels are short and pure, with *no glide*—that is, they are not diphthongs.

JAPANESE VOWEL	ENGLISH EQUIVALENT	EXAMPLE
a	as in father	akai (*ah-kah-ee*) red
e	as in men	ebi (*eh-bee*) shrimp
i	as in see	imi (*ee-mee*) meaning
o	as in boat	otoko (*oh-toh-koh*) male
u	as in food	uma (*oo-mah*) horse

15

The following vowels are like the ones you just saw, but lengthened.

JAPANESE VOWEL	ENGLISH EQUIVALENT	EXAMPLE
ā	as in f**a**ther, but lengthened	batā (bah-tah̄) butter
ei	as in m**e**n, but lengthened	e**i**go (eh̄-goh) English
ii	as in s**ee**, but lengthened	**ii**haru (ee̅-hah-roo) insist
ō	as in b**oa**t, but lengthened	ō**sama** (oh̄-sah-mah) king
ū	as in f**oo**d, but lengthened	yūbin (yoo̅-been) mail

Macrons

A *macron*, or bar, above a vowel means it should be lengthened.

   Example

   butter / batā / *bah-tah̄*

In the above word, the macron above the second vowel means you should hold the sound twice as long as you normally would.

And keep in mind these points:

• Long vowels are important. Pronouncing a long vowel incorrectly can result in a different word or even an unintelligible one.

   For example, obasan (*oh-bah-sahn*) means **aunt**
   obāsan (*oh-bah̄-sahn*) means **grandmother**

   ojisan (*oh-jee-sahn*) means **uncle**
   ojiisan (*oh-jee̅-sahn*) means **grandfather**

   seki (*seh-kee*) means **seat**
   seiki (*seh̄-kee*) means **century**

(For more examples, see **§19**.)

- Sometimes the **i** and the **u** aren't pronounced. This usually occurs between voiceless consonants (**p**, **t**, **k**, **ch**, **f**, **h**, **s**, **sh**), or at the end of a word following a voiceless consonant.

Examples

sukiyaki (*skee-yah-kee*)

This word for a popular Japanese dish begins with **skee**, not **soo**. The **u** is not pronounced.

tabemashita (*tah-beh-mahsh-tah*) **I ate**

The **i** is not pronounced.

§1.3
CONSONANTS

With a few exceptions, Japanese consonants are similar to those of English. Note those that are different:

f The English **f** is pronounced with a passage of air between the upper teeth and the lower lip. To make the Japanese **f**, blow air lightly between your lips as if you were just beginning a whistle.

g Always as in **go**, never as in a**ge**. You may also hear it pronounced as the **ng** sound in si**ng** but not at the beginning of a word.

r This is different from the English **r**. To make the Japanese **r**, lightly touch the tip of your tongue to the bony ridge behind the upper teeth, almost in the English **d** position. It's more like the Spanish **r**, but it's not trilled.

s Always hissed, as in **so**, never voiced, as in hi**s** or plea**s**ure.

And note the following points as well:

- If you have trouble making a consonant the Japanese way, your English pronunciation will still be intelligible.

- Some Japanese consonants are doubled. In English, this is just a feature of spelling and often doesn't affect pronunciation. In Japanese, the doubling is important and may change the meaning of a word.

Example

Kite kudasai (*kee-teh koo-dah-sah-ee*) means
"Please put it (clothing) on."

Kitte kudasai (*keet-teh koo-dah-sah-ee*) means
"Please cut it."

(For more examples, see **§20**.)

In a word with a doubled consonant, don't say the consonant twice—simply hold the sound longer.

§2.

The Japanese Writing System

§2.1 DIRECTION AND CHARACTERS

Traditionally, Japanese is written from top to bottom and from right to left. But it is also written horizontally and from left to right, as in English.

Japanese writing uses three kinds of characters:

kanji (*kahn-jee*)	漢字
hiragana (*hee-rah-gah-nah*)	ひらがな
katakana (*kah-tah-kah-nah*)	カタカナ

Hiragana and katakana are also called **kana** (*kah-nah*). All three are used together in Japanese writing.

§2.2 KANJI

Chinese and Japanese are completely different languages. But beginning in the fourth or fifth century, Japanese adopted written symbols and many vocabulary items from Chinese. In Japan, these symbols or Chinese characters are called **kanji**. They represent both meaning and sound, and often one kanji has more than one pronunciation (or reading, as it's commonly called) and meaning.

Japanese people learn about 2,000 kanji by the end of junior high school. Those are the basic characters used in newspapers, magazines, and school textbooks. Most Japanese know several thousand additional kanji as well.

Kanji range from simple, with one or two strokes, to complex, with many strokes needed to make one character. Some look like pictures, or line drawings, of the words they represent.

Examples

mountain	yama (*yah-mah*)	山
river	kawa (*kah-wah*)	川

19

These two together form Yamakawa, 山川 a family name. Here are some more kanji:

Japan	Nihon (*nee-hon*)	日本
person	hito (*hee-toh*)	人
	jin (*jeen*)	
Japanese	Nihonjin (*nee-hon-jeen*)	日本人

§2.3 HIRAGANA AND KATAKANA

Hiragana and **Katakana** symbols represent the sounds of syllables. Hiragana is used for native Japanese words and grammatical elements, and katakana is mainly for words of foreign origin. Each is a kind of alphabet, or syllabary, of 46 basic characters or sounds.

The following example will show you how the elements are used together.

Sumisu san, Nihon e yōkoso. / **Welcome to Japan, Mr. Smith.** スミスさん、日本へようこそ。

Smith	**Mr.**	**Japan**	**to welcome**	
|	|	|	|	|
Sumisu	san	Nihon	e	yōkoso
スミス	さん	日本	へ	ようこそ
katakana	hiragana	kanji		hiragana

The **hiragana** and **katakana** charts provided here will be useful if you continue your study of Japanese.

HIRAGANA

あ a (ah)	い i (ee)	う u (oo)	え e (eh)	お o (oh)
か ka (kah)	き ki (kee)	く ku (koo)	け ke (keh)	こ ko (koh)
さ sa (sah)	し shi (shee)	す su (soo)	せ se (seh)	そ so (soh)
た ta (tah)	ち chi (chee)	つ tsu (tsoo)	て te (teh)	と to (toh)
な na (nah)	に ni (nee)	ぬ nu (noo)	ね ne (neh)	の no (noh)
は ha (hah)	ひ hi (hee)	ふ fu (foo)	へ he (heh)	ほ ho (hoh)
ま ma (mah)	み mi (mee)	む mu (moo)	め me (meh)	も mo (moh)
や ya (yah)		ゆ yu (yoo)		よ yo (yoh)
ら ra (rah)	り ri (ree)	る ru (roo)	れ re (reh)	ろ ro (roh)
わ wa (wah)				を o (oh)
ん n				
が ga (gah)	ぎ gi (gee)	ぐ gu (goo)	げ ge (geh)	ご go (goh)
ざ za (zah)	じ ji (jee)	ず zu (zoo)	ぜ ze (zeh)	ぞ zo (zoh)
だ da (dah)	ぢ ji (jee)	づ zu (zoo)	で de (deh)	ど do (doh)
ば ba (bah)	び bi (bee)	ぶ bu (boo)	べ be (beh)	ぼ bo (boh)
ぱ pa (pah)	ぴ pi (pee)	ぷ pu (poo)	ぺ pe (peh)	ぽ po (poh)
きゃ kya (kyah)		きゅ kyu (kyoo)		きょ kyo (kyoh)
しゃ sha (shah)		しゅ shu (shoo)		しょ sho (shoh)
ちゃ cha (chah)		ちゅ chu (choo)		ちょ cho (choh)
にゃ nya (nyah)		にゅ nyu (nyoo)		にょ nyo (nyoh)
ひゃ hya (hyah)		ひゅ hyu (hyoo)		ひょ hyo (hyoh)
みゃ mya (myah)		みゅ myu (myoo)		みょ myo (myoh)
りゃ rya (ryah)		りゅ ryu (ryoo)		りょ ryo (ryoh)
ぎゃ gya (gyah)		ぎゅ gyu (gyoo)		ぎょ gyo (gyoh)
じゃ ja (jah)		じゅ ju (joo)		じょ jo (joh)
びゃ bya (byah)		びゅ byu (byoo)		びょ byo (byoh)
ぴゃ pya (pyah)		ぴゅ pyu (pyoo)		ぴょ pyo (pyoh)

KATAKANA

ア a (*ah*)	イ i (*ee*)	ウ u (*oo*)	エ e (*eh*)	オ o (*oh*)
カ ka (*kah*)	キ ki (*kee*)	ク ku (*koo*)	ケ ke (*keh*)	コ ko (*koh*)
サ sa (*sah*)	シ shi (*shee*)	ス su (*soo*)	セ se (*seh*)	ソ so (*soh*)
タ ta (*tah*)	チ chi (*chee*)	ツ tsu (*tsoo*)	テ te (*teh*)	ト to (*toh*)
ナ na (*nah*)	ニ ni (*nee*)	ヌ nu (*noo*)	ネ ne (*neh*)	ノ no (*noh*)
ハ ha (*hah*)	ヒ hi (*hee*)	フ fu (*foo*)	ヘ he (*heh*)	ホ ho (*hoh*)
マ ma (*mah*)	ミ mi (*mee*)	ム mu (*moo*)	メ me (*meh*)	モ mo (*moh*)
ヤ ya (*yah*)		ユ yu (*yoo*)		ヨ yo (*yoh*)
ラ ra (*rah*)	リ ri (*ree*)	ル ru (*roo*)	レ re (*reh*)	ロ ro (*roh*)
ワ wa (*wah*)				ヲ o (*oh*)

ン n				

ガ ga (*gah*)	ギ gi (*gee*)	グ gu (*goo*)	ゲ ge (*geh*)	ゴ go (*goh*)
ザ za (*zah*)	ジ ji (*jee*)	ズ zu (*zoo*)	ゼ ze (*zeh*)	ゾ zo (*zoh*)
ダ da (*dah*)	ヂ ji (*jee*)	ヅ zu (*zoo*)	デ de (*deh*)	ド do (*doh*)
バ ba (*bah*)	ビ bi (*bee*)	ブ bu (*boo*)	ベ be (*beh*)	ボ bo (*boh*)

パ pa (*pah*)	ピ pi (*pee*)	プ pu (*poo*)	ペ pe (*peh*)	ポ po (*poh*)
ファ fa (*fah*)	フィ fi (*fee*)	フ fu (*foo*)	フェ fe (*feh*)	フォ fo (*foh*)

キャ kya (*kyah*)		キュ kyu (*kyoo*)		キョ kyo (*kyoh*)
シャ sha (*shah*)		シュ shu (*shoo*)		ショ sho (*shoh*)
チャ cha (*chah*)		チュ chu (*choo*)		チョ cho (*choh*)
ニャ nya (*nyah*)		ニュ nyu (*nyoo*)		ニョ nyo (*nyoh*)
ヒャ hya (*hyah*)		ヒュ hyu (*hyoo*)		ヒョ hyo (*hyoh*)
ミャ mya (*myah*)		ミュ myu (*myoo*)		ミョ myo (*myoh*)
リャ rya (*ryah*)		リュ ryu (*ryoo*)		リョ ryo (*ryoh*)

ギャ gya (*gyah*)		ギュ gyu (*gyoo*)		ギョ gyo (*gyoh*)
ジャ ja (*jah*)		ジュ ju (*joo*)		ジョ jo (*joh*)
ビャ bya (*byah*)		ビュ byu (*byoo*)		ビョ byo (*byoh*)
ピャ pya (*pyah*)		ピュ pyu (*pyoo*)		ピョ pyo (*pyoh*)

**§2.4
ROMAJI**

The commonly used expression for the romanization of Japanese words is **romaji**. Although there are several systems of romaji, the most widely used, and the one used in this book, is a modified version of the Hepburn system.

§3.

Word Order

§3.1
WHAT IS A
SENTENCE?

A *sentence* is an organized series of words which enables us to make a statement, ask a question, express a thought, offer an opinion, and so forth. In writing, an English sentence starts with a capital letter and ends with a period, a question mark, or an exclamation mark. In writing (using romaji), a Japanese sentence starts with a capital letter, and ends with a period, not a question mark or an exclamation mark.

Examples

Yoko is Japanese. / Yōko san wa Nihonjin desu. (statement)

Is Yoko Japanese? / Yōko san wa Nihonjin desu ka. (question)

Yoko, be careful! / Yōko san ki o tsukete kudasai. (exclamation)

§3.2
THE ENGLISH
SENTENCE

English is a *Subject-Verb-Object* language. (So are French, German, Spanish, and Italian.) This means that in a typical sentence (a statement, not a question), the subject comes first, the verb next, and the object last. This kind of word order sequence for the sentence is sometimes referred to by the initials **SVO** (an SVO language).

Examples

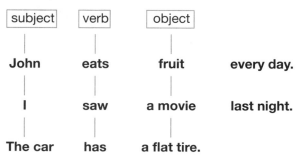

subject	verb	object	
John	eats	fruit	every day.
I	saw	a movie	last night.
The car	has	a flat tire.	

Understanding this principle of word order is important because, as we shall see in **§3.3**, the word order in Japanese is different.

24

English sentences have two basic parts, a *subject* and a *predicate*.

- The subject is "who" or "what" the sentence is about. A subject must contain a noun or pronoun. In a statement, the subject is usually the first element in the sentence.

  Examples

- The predicate is that part of the sentence that expresses what is said about the subject. It usually can be found directly after the subject, it must include a verb, and it includes everything remaining in the sentence that is not part of the subject.

  Examples

§3.3 THE JAPANESE SENTENCE

§3.3–1 Subject-Object-Verb Sentences

Japanese is a *Subject-Object-Verb* language. (So are Korean, Mongolian, and Turkish.) Thus, in a typical sentence, the subject comes first, the object next, and the verb last. This kind of word order sequence for the sentence is sometimes referred to by the initials **SOV** (an SOV language).

Examples

The significant difference from English here is that the verb must come at the *end* of the sentence.

- What about questions? The word order remains the same. But remember: Japanese does not use question marks. A sentence becomes a question by adding the particle *ka* at the end. You can think of *ka* as a question mark. (Particles, an important Part of Speech in Japanese, will be discussed in **§6**.)

Examples

**§3.3–2
Subject and
Predicate**

Japanese sentences *may* have a subject or a topic, but they *must* have a predicate. (The subject is followed by the particle *ga*, and the topic by the particle *wa*. See **§6**.)

- The *predicate* is the core of the Japanese sentence. It comes at the end, and it must be a verb or a verbal form. In Japanese, a verbal form may be a noun plus copula (like English **is** or **are**. See **§7.6**), or a verbal adjective.

Examples

- In addition to the *subject* or topic, there may, of course, be other elements in the sentence—*object*, *indirect object*, *adverb*, and so forth. They come before the predicate, and are not considered part of it.

- Two principles hold true for word order in a Japanese sentence:

  The predicate must come at the end of the sentence.

  A particle must immediately follow the word or words it marks.

- Other than this, word order is not rigid. The subject or topic usually comes first, although an adverb of time may precede it or follow it. Expressions of time usually precede expressions of place. Most modifiers precede the words they modify.

Examples

Kare   wa   mainichi   uchi   de   shinbun

he   topic   **every day home   at newspapers**
       marker

o   takusan yomimasu.

obj.   **many   reads**
marker

Kono kodomotachi   wa   Nihonjin   desu.

these   children   topic   **Japanese   are**
               marker

Shinbun   ga   tēburu no   ue   ni   arimasu.

newspaper subj.   **table   's   top   on (there) is**
          marker

Kyō   Jon san   wa   Tōkyō kara Kyōto ni ikimasu.

Today   John   topic   **from   to   will go**
               marker

Kanojo wa   honya   de   hon   o   kaimashita.

she topic   **bookstore at book** obj.   **bought**
        marker   marker

- With a question, the word order is the same. As you now know, the particle *ka* at the end of the sentence makes a statement into a question.

Example

Kanojo wa honya de hon o kaimashita ka. / **Did she buy a book at the bookstore?**

she topic
        marker

• If a question uses a question word (*when*, *who*, *what*, etc.), it normally comes after the subject or topic, but this is not rigid.

Examples

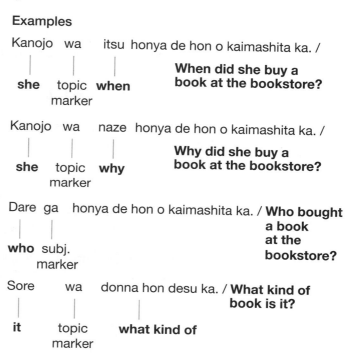

Kanojo wa itsu honya de hon o kaimashita ka. /
she | topic | when
marker
When did she buy a book at the bookstore?

Kanojo wa naze honya de hon o kaimashita ka. /
she | topic | why
marker
Why did she buy a book at the bookstore?

Dare ga honya de hon o kaimashita ka. / **Who bought a book at the bookstore?**
who | subj.
marker

Sore wa donna hon desu ka. / **What kind of book is it?**
it | topic | what kind of
marker

§3.3–3 Incomplete Sentences

In most languages, words that can be understood or implied from the context of the situation can be left out of a sentence. In Japanese, it is the subject or topic that is omitted, not the predicate. If the situation is clear without the subject or topic, Japanese tend to leave it out.

Example

Kore wa nan desu ka. / **What is this?**
    Kore wa hon desu. / **This is a book.**
    or
    Hon desu.
    book | is

In English, this question could be answered with just the noun: **A book.**

In Japanese, the copula, or verb **to be** is needed too. Remember, a Japanese sentence must have a predicate, or verb form. Look at some more examples.

Example

Anata wa   nani o   kaimashita ka. / **What did you buy?**

you	**what**	**did buy**

Although this sentence is gramatically correct, the Japanese prefer to omit the **you** which would be obvious from the context.

Example

Nani o kaimashita ka. / **What did (you) buy?**

Hon o kaimashita. / **(I) bought a book.**

In a sense, these shouldn't be called "incomplete sentences" because, to the Japanese, they are quite complete!

Parts of Speech

§4.

Nouns

A *noun* is a word that names or refers to a person, a place, or a thing. A thing may be a quality or a concept.

There are two main types of nouns:

- A *proper* noun names a particular person, place, or thing. In English, all proper nouns are capitalized. The Japanese concept of proper nouns is more limited. In romaji (see §2.4), names of persons or places, for example, are capitalized, but days of the week and months of the year are not. The words for other languages are capitalized, but not the word for English: *eigo*.

Examples

31

• A *common* noun does not name a particular person, place, or thing.

Examples

hon / **book**   otokonoko / **boy**   onnanoko / **girl**

§4.2 GENDER

Japanese nouns do not have *gender*. There are no special endings to show masculine, feminine, or neuter forms.

§4.3 ARTICLES

Japanese does not use *articles* before nouns. There are no words to correspond to English **a**, **an**, or **the**.

§4.4 NUMBER

Number means that a word can be *singular* (referring to one person, thing, etc.) or *plural* (referring to more than one). With most Japanese nouns, number is not an issue. *The same word is used for one or for more than one.*

Examples

hon / **book, books**   uchi / **house, houses**

shinbun / **newspaper,**   ki / **tree, trees**
    newspapers   te / **hand, hands**

kuruma / **car, cars**

Hon o motte imasu. / **I have a book.**

Hon o motte imasu. / **I have some books.**

• For nouns referring to people, the plural suffix *-tachi* may be used, although it isn't required.

Examples

kodomo / **child, children**   kodomotachi / **children**
otokonoko / **boy, boys**   otokonokotachi / **boys**
onnanoko / **girl, girls**   onnanokotachi / **girls**
hahaoya / **mother, mothers**   hahaoyatachi / **mothers**
sensei / **teacher, teachers**   senseitachi / **teachers**

• When -*tachi* is used with someone's name, it usually refers to the person and his or her family or group.

Examples

Tanaka san tachi / **Mr. Tanaka and his family**

Tomoko san tachi / **Tomoko and her group**

§4.5
NAMES

Japanese use *family names first*, and *first names last*.

Examples

When Japanese introduce themselves to each other, they say the family name first. However, they know that English speakers do it the opposite way.

Japanese prefer family names, not first names. Japanese adults rarely use first names. Even among friends, family names are the rule, first names the exception. Unless a Japanese specifically asks you to use his or her first name, you should use the family name.

With children, it's different. Japanese use young children's first names followed by the title *chan*, older children's first names followed by *san* (see **§4.6**).

Sometimes *kun* is used for boys instead of *chan*. The switch from *chan* to *san* or *kun* occurs around 10 years of age, or the start of junior high school.

§4.6
TITLES

The Japanese word that corresponds to English **Mr.**, **Mrs.**, **Miss**, and **Ms.** is *san*. The Japanese always use *san* (or other, more formal titles of respect) with proper names. Even among family members or close personal friends who use first names with each other, *san* follows the name.

Be sure to use *san* in direct address (when speaking directly to someone), and when referring to someone else. *Never* use *san* to refer to yourself.

Examples

Tanaka san, kōhī wa ikaga desu ka. / **Mr. Tanaka, would you like some coffee?**

Merī san wa, kyō gakkō ni imasu ka. / **Is Mary at school today?**

But note the following:

Watakushi wa, John Smith desu. / **I'm John Smith.**

§4.7 POLITENESS

The prefix *o-* before certain nouns expresses *politeness*. (This is also used with verbs and adjectives. See **§7** and **§8**.)

Examples

namae, onamae / **name**	kane, okane / **money**
sake, osake / **rice wine**	furo, ofuro / **bath**
hashi, ohashi / **chopsticks**	tegami, otegami / **letter**

A variation of this form is *go-*, which is used with words of Chinese origin.

hon, gohon / **book**   kekkon, gokekkon / **marriage**

Note the following about the prefixes *o-* and *go-*:

* Although both men and women may use the above forms, in some cases, these prefixes would be used only by women, as in the "o" forms in examples below.

Examples

niku, oniku / **meat**   yasai, oyasai / **vegetables**

* Some words are *always* used with the polite prefix. The *o-* and *go-* are now part of the words:

Examples

ocha / **Japanese tea**   gohan / **cooked rice, meal**

These prefixes cannot be used with all nouns. It's best to use them only when you are certain they are correct, as with the previous examples.

§4.8 COMPOUND NOUNS

When two nouns are used together to make a *compound noun*, they are usually joined by the particle *no*.

Examples

rekishi no kurasu / **history class**

eigo no sensei / **English teacher**

apāto no biru / **apartment building**

Some compound nouns may be formed *without* the *no*, however.

Examples

kōhī jawan / **coffee cup**

kankō basu / **tour bus**

bōeki gaisha / **trading company**

§4.9 NOUN SUFFIXES

- The suffix -*ya*, when added to a noun, means the place or shop where that thing is sold, or the person or shopkeeper who sells it.

Examples

niku / **meat**   ⟶   nikuya / **butcher shop, butcher**

hon / **book**   ⟶   honya / **bookstore, clerk, owner**

kamera / **camera** ⟶ kameraya / **camera shop, clerk, owner**

- When referring to the clerk or shopkeeper, the title *san* is used:

Examples

nikuya san / **butcher**

kameraya san / **camera shop clerk**

- The suffix -*ka*, when added to a noun, means a person with expertise or special knowledge on that subject.

Examples

seiji / **politics**   ⟶ seijika / **politician**

hyōron / **commentary** ⟶ hyōronka / **critic, commentator**

shōsetsu / **novel**   ⟶ shōsetsuka / **novelist**

geijutsu / **art**   ⟶ geijutsuka / **artist**

§5.

Pronouns

A *pronoun* is a word that takes the place of a noun. Here are some common English pronouns: **I, you, he, she, it, we, they**. These are personal pronouns used as *subjects*. Other common English pronouns are **me, him, her, us, them**. These are personal pronouns used as *objects*. **You** and **it**, of course, may be subjects or objects. In addition to these, there are other kinds of pronouns, such as *possessive* (**mine, yours, his**, etc.), *demonstrative* (**this, that**), and *interrogative* (**who, where, what**, etc.)

Japanese pronoun usage is quite different from that of English, as you will see from the following discussion.

§5.2
PERSONAL
PRONOUNS

Personal pronouns in Japanese refer to people, not things or ideas. Japanese has no equivalent to the English **it** in this category.

When the meaning can be understood from the context, the Japanese prefer *not* to use personal pronouns. Use these with care, and be sure to read the information that follows.

Singular	Plural
watakushi / **I, me**	watakushitachi / **we, us**
anata / **you**	anatatachi / **you** anatagata / **you** (polite)
kare / **he, him**	karera / **they, them** (all male or male and female)
kanojo / **she, her**	kanojotachi / **they, them** (female) kanojora / **they, them** (female)

Informal usage

watashi / **I, me**

atashi / **I, me** (female)

§5.2–1
Special Usage

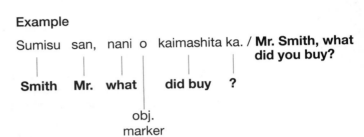

anata / **you**

Avoid using this whenever possible. When speaking to someone directly, try to use the person's name and *san* instead.

Example

Sumisu san, nani o kaimashita ka. / **Mr. Smith, what did you buy?**

Smith   Mr.   what   did buy   ?

obj.
marker

- When speaking to a teacher, a doctor, a dentist, or a member of the Diet (the Japanese legislature), use the word *sensei*, either alone, or after the person's last name. *Sensei*, which literally means "teacher," may also be used with others not listed above. A teacher can be one who has achieved success or earned respect in his or her field. You can use *sensei*, for example, to address an artist, writer, architect, musician, or other talented person.

Example

Sensei, ogenki desu ka. / **Sir (teacher), how have you been?**

If you are speaking to a group, you can use the following expressions for "you" (plural):

Example

mina san / **everyone (you all)**   mina sama / **everyone (you all)**

mina / **everyone** + san

or

sama (very polite, and more formal than *san*)

Examples

Mina san, ohayō gozaimasu. / **Good morning, everyone.**

Mina sama, sayōnara. / **Goodbye, everyone!**

kare / **he**	kanojo / **she**

- Whenever possible, when referring to a third person, use the person's name.

Example

Sumisu san wa Nyūyōku kara kimashita ka. / **Is Mrs. Smith from New York?**

This is better than saying, "Is *she* from New York?" Of course, if it is clear who the subject is, it can be left out entirely.

- Several other terms can be used instead of the pronouns *kare*, *kanojo*, and their plural forms. The Japanese prefer these:

Singular	Plural
ano hito / **that person**	ano hitotachi / **those persons**
ano kata / **that person (polite)**	ano katagata / **those persons (polite)**

Examples

Kinō |ano hito| ni aimashita ka. / **Did you see him (that person) yesterday?**

that person

|Ano katagata| wa kinō irasshaimashita. / **They (those persons) were here yesterday.**

those persons

§5.2–2
Case

Case refers to the form of a pronoun which shows its relationship to other words in a sentence.

In English, the personal pronouns have three cases: the *nominative* (used for the subject of a sentence or clause), the *objective* (used for the object of a sentence, indirect object, or object of a preposition), and the *possessive* (showing ownership). English has a different set of personal pronouns for each of these cases.

Examples

He lives here.	*He* = nominative case (subject of the sentence)
I see *him*.	*him* = objective case (object of the verb)
His car is here.	*His* = possessive case (shows ownership)

In Japanese, the personal pronouns function with all three cases, but the words stay the same. The case is shown by a *particle*, or postposition, that comes after the pronoun. Note that in the following examples of how one pronoun, *watakushi*, is used for different grammatical functions, the topic marker *wa*, rather than the subject marker *ga*, is preferred. This will be discussed in more detail in the chapter on Particles (see **§6**).

Examples

§5.3 INTERROGATIVE PRONOUNS

Although some are pronouns and some are other parts of speech in Japanese, these are all interrogative words.

dare / **who**
dō / **how**
doko / **where** (place)
donna / **what kind of**
dochira / **where, which** (direction, preference)
dore / **which** (persons, things)
dotchi / **which** (of two choices)
donata / **which person, who** (polite)
dōshite / **why**
naze / **why**
nan, nani / **what**
nannin / **how many people**
ikura / **how much**
ikutsu / **how many**
itsu / **when**

§5.4 INDEFINITE PRONOUNS

dareka / **someone**	daremo / **no one**
donataka / **someone** (polite)	donatamo / **no one** (polite)
doreka / **something**	doremo / **nothing**
dokoka / **somewhere**	dokomo / **nowhere**
nanika / **something**	nanimo / **nothing**
ikuraka / **some, a little**	ikuramo / **not much**
nandemo / **anything**	nannimo / **nothing**

• Note that the expressions listed on the right side of the preceding chart take *negative* verbs in order to have a negative meaning.

Examples

Dareka   kimashita. / **Someone came.**

someone   **came**

Daremo   kimasen deshita. / **No one came.**

no one   **didn't come**

§5.5 DEMONSTRATIVE PRONOUNS

The *demonstrative* words (some are pronouns and some are adjectives or adverbs) form a pattern of prefixes:

ko- / **here** (close to the speaker)
so- / **there** (away from the speaker)
a- / **over there** (some distance from the speaker)
do- / **question**

The last one, *do-*, can be seen in **§5.3**.

Here are the rest:

	ko- / **here**	so- / **there**	a- / **over there**
Pronoun	kore / **this**	sore / **that**	are / **that**
Adjective	kono / **this**	sono / **that**	ano / **that**
Adjective	konna / **this kind of**	sonna / **that kind of**	anna / **that kind of**
Adverb	kō / **in this manner**	sō / **in that manner**	ā/ **in that manner**
Adverb, Pronoun	koko / **here**	soko / **there**	asoko / **over there**
Adverb, Pronoun	kochira / **here, this**	sochira / **there, that**	achira / **there, that**

This form is politer usage than the one above.

§5.6 RELATIVE PRONOUNS

The *relative* pronouns in English are **who, whom, whose, which, where,** and **that**. Because relative clauses in Japanese precede, rather than follow, the words they modify, Japanese does not have words that correspond to these pronouns.

Example

Kyō tsuita hito wa Yamada san desu. / **The man who arrived today is Mr. Yamada.**

today | man | arrived | topic marker | is

Notice that the Japanese sentence has no word to correspond to the relative pronoun "who" in the English sentences.

This will be explained further in the section on Verbs (see **§7**).

§5.7 REFLEXIVE PRONOUNS

The *reflexive* pronouns in English are words such as **myself, yourself, himself, yourselves,** and so forth. Japanese has only one word to correspond to these pronouns. You might call it an all-purpose reflexive pronoun. Its meaning is both singular and plural, masculine and feminine. It can be used for humans and for warm-blooded animals. It cannot be used for fish, reptiles, insects, or inanimate objects.

> jibun / **one's self**

This is commonly followed by particles such as *de* or *no* (see **§6**).

Examples

Jibun de ikimasu. / **I'm going myself.**

Jibun de shinasai. / **Do it yourself.**

Jibun no koto wa jibun de shinasai. / **Do your own work by yourself.**

Merī san wa, jibun de benkyō shite imasu. / **Mary is studying by herself.**

§6.

Particles

§6.1 WHAT ARE PARTICLES?

A particle is a word that shows the relationship of a word, a phrase, or a clause to the rest of the sentence. Some particles show grammatical function—subject, object, indirect object. Some have meaning themselves, like English prepositions. But since they always *follow* the word or words they mark, they are *post*positions.

The lists that follow include some of the more common particles, and some of their uses.

§6.2 PARTICLES USED WITH WORDS OR PHRASES

wa	de	made ni
ga	e	mo
o	hodo	shika
no	ka	to
ni	kara	ya
dake	made	yori

wa

topic marker

How do you decide if an expression is a topic, marked with *wa*, or a subject, marked with *ga*? Both look like the subject of an English sentence!

Think of the topic as a comment on something that has already been introduced into the conversation, or that is part of general or shared knowledge. As such, *wa* can mean

"Speaking of (the) . . ." or "As for (the)."

Examples

Kimura san wa,   gakusei   desu. / **Mr. Kimura is a**
                                    student. (Speaking of
                                    Mr. Kimura, he's a
        topic **student**   **is**   **student.)**
        marker

Nihonjin wa,   hashi   o tsukaimasu. / **The Japanese use chopsticks. (As for the Japanese, they use chopsticks.)**

chopsticks   use

topic   obj.
marker   marker

- Note that *wa* as a topic marker can also follow what in English may look like an object, a phrase, or a clause.

Examples

Asagohan wa   hachiji ni tabemashita. / **I ate breakfast at 8 o'clock. (Speaking of breakfast, I ate at 8 o'clock.)**

breakfast topic   **8**   **at**   **ate**
marker **o'clock**

Hachiji ni   wa asagohan o   tabemashita.

8   **at** topic   object
o'clock   marker   marker

/ **I ate breakfast at 8 o'clock. (Speaking of 8 o'clock, I ate breakfast then.)**

Asagohan o tabeta no   wa   hachiji deshita. / **I ate breakfast at 8 o'clock. (The time I ate breakfast was 8 o'clock.)**

ate   topic   **was**
marker
nominalizer

contrast

Wa can follow a noun to show contrast. The thing being contrasted may or may not be stated, but with this usage, the contrast is implied.

Examples

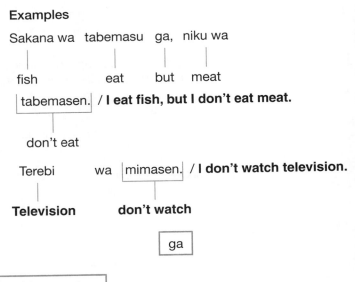

Sakana wa tabemasu ga, niku wa

fish   eat   but   meat

tabemasen. / **I eat fish, but I don't eat meat.**

don't eat

Terebi   wa   mimasen. / **I don't watch television.**

Television   **don't watch**

ga

subject marker

Ga marks what the Japanese call the grammatical *subject* of a sentence. Think of the subject in the following two ways:

- First, in neutral descriptions of observable actions or situations.

Examples

Tegami   ga   kimashita. / **The mail came.**

mail   subj.   **came**
          marker

Ame   ga   futte imasu. / **It's raining. (The rain is falling.)**

rain subj.   **is falling**
        marker

Note that in the negative counterparts of these sentences, *wa*, not *ga*, must be used.

Tegami wa kimasen deshita. / **The mail didn't come.**

- Second, for special emphasis, to distinguish a particular person or thing from all others.

Examples

Watakushi ga shimashita. / **I did it. (I am the one who did it.)**

Tōkyō ga ōkii desu. / **Tokyo is big. (It is Tokyo that is big.)**

- When an interrogative pronoun is used as the subject of a sentence, *ga* must always be used too.

Example

Dare   ga,   kore   o   shimashita   ka. / **Who did this? (Who is the one who did this?)**

| | | | | |
| **who** | subj. marker | **this** | obj. marker | **did** | **?** |

---

object marker

O usually marks the object. But *ga* marks the object of certain non-action verbs and certain verbal adjectives and adjectival nouns (see **§8**).

Examples

Yōko san wa,   eigo   ga   wakarimasu. / **Yoko understands English.**

| topic marker | **English** | obj. marker | **understands** |

Nihongo   ga   dekimasu ka. / **Can you speak Japanese?**

| obj. marker | **can do?** |

Hon   ga   hoshii desu. / **I want a book.**

| **book** | obj. marker | **want** |

Merī san wa, tenisu ga   jōzu desu. / **Mary is good at tennis.**

topic   obj.   **good at is**
marker   marker

o

direct object marker

Examples

Senshū   sono   hon o yomimashita. / **I read that book last week.**

last week that book   read

Jon san wa eiga o mimashita. / **John saw a movie.**

movie   saw

through, along, in

The particle *o* is used with verbs such as **walk**, **run**, **drive**, **go through**, etc., when speaking of continuous motion and a finite place or distance.

Examples

Tanaka san wa, Chūō Dōri o arukimashita. / **Mr. Tanaka walked along Central Avenue.**

Central Avenue   walked

Kōen o hashirimashita. / **I ran through the park.**

park   ran

no

possessive marker

Think of this like the English apostrophe plus **s**.

Examples

Watakushi no | inu wa, pūdoru desu. / **My dog is a poodle.**

My   dog   poodle   is

Kodomo no | kao ga yogorete imasu. / **The child's face is dirty.**

Child's   face   dirty   is

noun modification

This usage of *no* is similar to the possessive, but it is seen more with compound nouns or noun phrases.

Examples

Sūgaku no | kurasu wa, muzukashii desu. / **The math class is difficult.**

math   class   difficult   is

Amerika no | tabemono wa, oishii desu. / **American food is delicious.**

American   food   delicious is

appositional

No links the noun or pronoun to the appositive that follows.

Examples

Nikuya no | Doi san | wa, okanemochi desu. / **The butcher, Mr. Doi, is rich.**

The butcher Mr. Doi   rich   is

Amerikajin no Jon san wa, Shikago kara

John, the American   **from**

kimashita. / **The American, John, is from Chicago.**

came

• For the nominalization use of *no*, see **§7.19** and **§8.5**.

ni

indirect object marker

Examples

Yamada san ni hanashimashita. / **I talked to Ms. Yamada.**

to   **talked**

Hon o watakushi ni kudasai. / **Please give me the book. (Please give the book to me.)**

book   **me**   **to please give**

• Note that some Japanese verbs, such as **ask** and **meet**, take an indirect object, although their English counterparts do not.

Examples

Watakushi wa, Tanaka san ni kikimashita. / **I asked Mr. Tanaka.**

to   **asked**

Tomodachi ni aimashita. / **I met my friend.**

friend   **to**   **met**

location

With stative (non-action) verbs meaning **there is/are**, *imasu* for people, *arimasu* for things, *ni* means **in**, **at**, or **on**, and so forth.

Examples

Merī san wa, Kyōto ni imasu. / **Mary is in Kyoto.**

Ginza wa Tōkyō ni arimasu. / **Ginza is in Tokyo.**

Haha wa depāto ni imasu. / **My mother is at the department store.**

| | |
my   department
mother   store

For location, the equivalents of English expressions **near**, **under**, **inside**, **on top of**, etc., are useful. Note how they are formed in Japanese. First look at the following words:

ue / **top**	shita / **bottom**
mae / **front**	ushiro / **back**
naka / **inside**	soto / **outside**
chikaku / **nearby**	tonari / **next to**
yoko / **side**	

These words are nouns in Japanese. To form a locational phrase, the particle *no* links another noun to one of these, and then the particle *ni* follows.

tēburu   no   ue   ni / **on top of the table**

| | | |
table   's   top on

Hon wa, tēburu no ue ni arimasu. / **The book is on top of the table.**

uchi   no   naka   ni / **inside the house**

| | | |
house 's   inside in

Jon san wa, uchi no naka ni imasu. / **John is inside the house.**

eki　no　chikaku　ni / **near the station**

station's　　nearby　at

Yūbinkyoku wa, eki no chikaku ni arimasu. / **The post office is near the station.**

> direction

With verbs of motion, *ni* means **to** or **toward**.

Examples

Nakamura san wa, | mainichi | Tōkyō

every day

ni ikimasu. / **Mrs. Nakamura goes to Tokyo every day.**

to goes

Ano hito | wa, Amerika ni kaerimashita. / **He returned to America.**

He　　　　　　　　　　　to　returned

> specific time

With expressions of specific time, *ni* means **at** (clock time), **in** (month, year), or **on** (day).

Examples

ichiji ni / **at one o'clock**
gogo jūichiji ni / **at 11 P.M.**

Ano hitotachi | wa, | shichiji han | ni tsukimashita. / **They arrived at 7:30.**

They　　　　　　　　7:30　　at　arrived

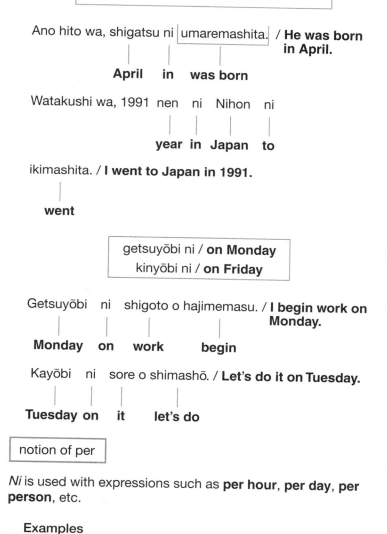

> rokugatsu ni / **in June**
> kugatsu ni / **in September**
> nisenhachi nen ni / **in (the year) 2008**

Ano hito wa, shigatsu ni umaremashita. / **He was born in April.**

April	**in**	**was born**

Watakushi wa, 1991 nen ni Nihon ni

	year	**in**	**Japan**	**to**

ikimashita. / **I went to Japan in 1991.**

went

> getsuyōbi ni / **on Monday**
> kinyōbi ni / **on Friday**

Getsuyōbi ni shigoto o hajimemasu. / **I begin work on Monday.**

Monday **on** **work** **begin**

Kayōbi ni sore o shimashō. / **Let's do it on Tuesday.**

Tuesday **on** **it** **let's do**

notion of per

Ni is used with expressions such as **per hour**, **per day**, **per person**, etc.

Examples

ichijikan ni san doru / **three dollars per hour**

hour **per** **three** **dollars**

Isshūkan ni yonjūhachi jikan hatarakimasu. / **I work 48 hours a week.**

| | | | | |
| week | per | 48 | hours | work |

Sandoitchi o hitori ni futatsu tsukurimasu.

| | | | | |
| **Sandwiches** | **person** | **per** | **two** | **will make** |

/ **I'll make two sandwiches per person.**

For some other uses of *ni*, see §7.12 and §7.13.

dake

limitation

Dake translates English words such as **only**, **all**, **just**, **no more than**, **as many as**, and **as much as**.

Examples

Sore dake desu ka. / **Is that all?**

| | | | |
| **that** | **all** | **is** | **?** |

Terebi wa, nyūsu bangumi dake mimasu. / **On television I watch only the news.**

| | | | |
| **news** | **program** | **only** | **watch** |

Suki na dake tabete kudasai. / **Please eat as much as you want.**

| | | | |
| **want** | **as much as** | **eat** | **please** |

de

place of action

This use of *de* means **in**, **at**, **on**, and so forth. It is used with action verbs, or with *arimasu* when action is implied.

Example

Panya   de   kaimashita. / **I bought it at the bakery.**

  | | |

bakery **at** **bought**

> means

De translates **by**, or **by means of**, **with**, **in**, etc.

Examples

Takushī   de   ikimashita. / **I went by taxi.**

 | | |

taxi **by** **went**

Jisho   de   shirabemashita. / **I checked it in the**
             dictionary.

 | | |

dictionary **in** **checked**

> totalizing

This use of *de* connotes a **unit**, a **certain number** or **amount**, or **together**.

Examples

futari de / **(by) two people**

Futari de shimasu. / **Two of us (together) will do it.**

      |

     will do

Nihon   ni | futari de | ikimasu. / **Two of us will go**
            to Japan.

 | | | |

Japan **to** **two people** **will go**

| Zenbu de | sen   en   desu. / **All together it's**
            1,000 yen.

  | | | |

all together **1,000** **yen** **is**

| time limit |

The meaning of *de* here is **within** or **in** for a given length of time.

Examples

Nishūkan   de   dekimasu. / **I can do it within two weeks.**

two weeks   **within**   **can do**

Ichijikan   de   ikemasu. / **You can go in one hour.**

one hour   **in**   **can go**

| scope |

Here *de* means **among**, **of**, **within**, etc., referring to extent or range.

Examples

Kudamono   de,   nani ga   ichiban   suki desu   ka.

fruit   **of**   **which**   **most**   **like**   **?**

/ **Which of the fruit do you like the most?**

Amerika   de,   doko   ni   ikitai desu   ka. / **Where in America do you want to go?**

    within   **where**   **want to go**   **?**   go?

| material |

Here *de* means **of** or **from** in **made of** or **made from** expressions.

Examples

Kono tēburu wa,   ki   de   dekite imasu. / **This table is made of wood.**

    table   **wood**   **of**   **is made**

Kore wa, gin de tsukurimashita. / **I made it of silver.**

silver of   made

| e |

| direction |

Like *ni, e* is used with verbs of motion to indicate **to** or **toward**.

Example

Kariforunia e | ikimasu | ka. / **Are you going to California?**

are going

| hodo |

| extent or degree |

Hodo means **as much as**, or **as . . . as**, and it is often used in negative constructions, although the meaning is positive.

Examples

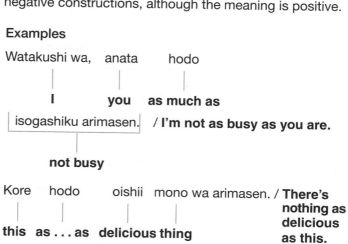

Watakushi wa, anata hodo

I   **you**   **as much as**

| isogashiku arimasen. | / **I'm not as busy as you are.**

not busy

Kore hodo oishii mono wa arimasen. / **There's nothing as delicious as this.**

this as . . . as delicious thing

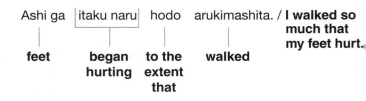

Ashi ga │itaku naru│ hodo   arukimashita. / **I walked so much that my feet hurt.**

feet   began   to the   walked
             hurting   extent
                            that

---

about, approximately

With things that can be counted, *hodo* means **about** or **approximately**.

Examples

Sen   en   hodo   desu. / **It's about 1,000 yen.**

1,000   yen   about   is

Isshūkan   hodo   de   │dekimasu.│   / **It can be done in about a week.**

a week   about   in   can be done

ka

---

enumerative

The meaning of *ka* here is **or**, that is, listing parallel things and then choosing.

Examples

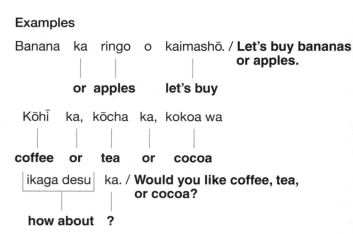

Banana   ka   ringo   o   kaimashō. / **Let's buy bananas or apples.**

or   apples   let's buy

Kōhī   ka,   kōcha   ka,   kokoa wa

coffee   or   tea   or   cocoa

│ikaga desu│   ka. / **Would you like coffee, tea, or cocoa?**

how about   ?

- Note that *ka*, like many particles, has several meanings. In the previous example, it is also used as the question marker at the end of the sentence.

kara

place of departure, origin

The meaning of *kara* here is **from**.

Examples

Kono kisha wa, Kyōto kara kimashita. / **This train came from Kyoto.**
this train from came

Watakushi wa, Nihon kara kimashita. / **I am from Japan.**
I from

starting time

The meaning of *kara* here would be expressed by **at** in English, but in Japanese, the meaning is **from a certain time and continuing on**. In other words, it is the beginning of a period of time. It differs from the use of the particle *ni*, which means **at a precise time. (Meet me at one o'clock.)**

Examples

Gēmu wa, ichiji kara hajimarimasu. / **The game begins at one o'clock.**
game one o'clock from begins

Getsuyōbi kara isogashiku narimasu. / **Starting Monday, I'll be busy.**
Monday from busy become

source

Kara also means **from** in the sense of **origin**.

Examples

Tanaka san   kara   kikimashita. / **I heard it from Mrs. Tanaka.**
           | |
         from   **heard**

Kono   hon wa, toshokan   kara   karimashita. / **I borrowed this book from the library.**
 | | | | |
this book   library   from   borrowed

made

target time or place

Made means **until**, **as far as**. It is often combined with *kara* in a sentence.

Example

Yūgata   made | benkyō shimashita. | / **I studied until evening.**
 | | |
evening until   studied

Tsugi   no kado | made | arukimashō. | / **Let's walk as far as the next corner.**
 | | | |
next   corner as far as let's walk

Gakkō wa,   kuji   kara   sanji   made
 | | | | |
school   9 o'clock   from   3 o'clock   until

desu. / **School is from 9 until 3 o'clock.**
 |
is

made ni

time limit

Unlike the time limit usage of the particle *de* (**within**), *made ni* means **by** (the time given), or **not later than**.

Examples

Goji | made ni | dekimasu | ka. / **Can you do it by 5 o'clock?**
5 o'clock **by** **can do**

Kayōbi | made ni | hitsuyō desu. | / **I need it by Tuesday.**
Tuesday **by** **need**

mo

including, excluding

Mo means **also** or **too**. Depending on which word it follows in a sentence, *mo* can replace *wa*, *ga*, or *o*. When used with a negative verb, the meaning is **(not) either**, or **neither . . . nor**.

Examples

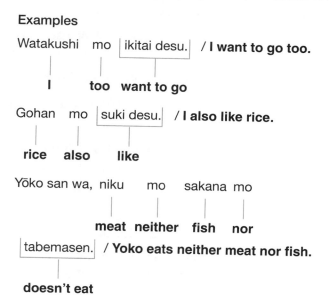

Watakushi mo | ikitai desu. | / **I want to go too.**
I **too** **want to go**

Gohan mo | suki desu. | / **I also like rice.**
rice **also** **like**

Yōko san wa, niku mo sakana mo
meat neither fish nor
tabemasen. | / **Yoko eats neither meat nor fish.**
doesn't eat

emphasis

This meaning of *mo* is **even** in the sense of emphasis.

Examples

Ano Amerikajin wa,   sashimi   mo

raw fish   **even**

tabemasu. / **That American even eats raw fish.**

eats

Ichi   doru   mo | arimasen. | / **I don't even have one dollar.**

one   **dollar**   **even**   **there isn't**

shika

limitation

Shika means **only, just**. Although the meaning is affirmative, it takes the negative form of the verb.

Examples

Eigo   shika   shirimasen. / **I only know English.**

English   **only**   **don't know**

Shinbun   shika   yomimasen. / **I only read newspapers.**

newspapers   **only**   **don't read**

to

complete listing

To means **and** when stating all possible items in a list. The implication is **and nothing more**.

Examples

Jon san to Merī san ga kimashita. / **John and Mary came.**

Enpitsu   to,   nōto   to, jōgi o kaimashita.

pencils and notebook and ruler   bought

/ **I bought pencils, a notebook, and a ruler.**

involvement

Here, *to* means **together with**.

Examples

Satō san to   honya   e ikimashita. / **I went to the bookstore with Mr. Sato.**

with bookstore to   went

Tomu san to   issho ni   hon o kakimashita. / **I wrote a book with Tom.**

with together book   wrote

quotation

To follows both direct and indirect quotations.

Examples

Ono san wa, "Watakushi ga shimasu" to iimashita.

I   will do   said

/ **"I'll do it," said Mr. Ono.**

Ono san wa, kare ga   suru   to iimashita. / **Mr. Ono said that he would do it.**

he   would do   said

ya

partial listing

Ya is used for **and** when stating a sample of, or some of the items in, a list. The implication is **and others**, **among others**, or **such things as**; that is, something has been left out.

Examples

Jon san ya Merī san ga kimashita. / **John, Mary, and others came.**

Enpitsu ya,   nōto   ya,   jōgi o   kaimashita.
| | | | | |
pencil and notebook and   ruler   bought

/ **I bought such things as a pencil, a notebook, and a ruler.**

yori

comparison

Used when comparing things, *yori* means **than**. Think of it as the **than** in expressions such as **bigger than**, **smaller than**, **better than**, **worse than**, **rather than**, etc. It is often used in combination with *hō* (contrast) (see **§8**).

Examples

Kore   yori   sore   o kudasai. / **Please give me that rather than this.**
| | | |
this   rather than   that   please give

Pan   yori   gohan no hō ga │suki desu.│
| | |
bread   more than   rice   like

/ **I like rice more than bread.**

Kyōto wa, Tōkyō yori   samui   desu. / **Kyoto is colder than Tokyo.**

| | |
more than   cold   is

Amerika wa, Nihon yori   ōkii   desu. / **America is larger than Japan.**

more than   large   is

§6.3 PARTICLES USED WITH CLAUSES

ga	node
kara	noni
keredo	to
nagara	

| ga |

| contrary reasoning |

Ga means **but**, **even though**, or **although**. The implication is **despite the circumstances**.

Examples

Samui   desu   ga,   dekakemashita. / **Although it's cold, I went out.**

cold   is although   went out

Byōki desu ga, shigoto ni ikimasu. / **I'm sick, but I'm going to work.**

sick   am but   work   to   go

• *Ga* is often used at the end of a clause with the final clause implied but unsaid. This has a softening effect on the exchange, with both speakers understanding the meaning of what has been left unspoken.

Examples

| Ikitakatta desu | ga ...   / **I wanted to go but ... (I couldn't).**

wanted to go   but

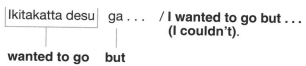

neutral connector

Here, *ga* means **and**.

Examples

Hawai ni ikimashita ga, | subarashikatta desu. | / **I went to Hawaii, and it was wonderful.**

went   **and**   **was wonderful**

Sono hon o yomimashita ga, | omoshirokatta desu. |

read   **and**   **was interesting**

/ **I read that book, and it was interesting.**

kara

reason

Here, *kara* means **because** or **since**.

Examples

Isogashii kara ikemasen. / **Because I'm busy, I can't go.**

busy   **because** **can't go**

Ame da kara uchi ni imasu. / **Since it's raining, I'll stay home.**

rain **is** **since** **home** **at** **stay**

sequential action

The meaning of *kara* here is **after**, **since**, **ever since**.

Examples

Tabete kara shigoto o shimasu. / **After eating, I'll do some work.**

eating   **after** **work**   **will do**

| Kekkonshite | | kara | shiawase | desu. | / **Ever since he got married, he has been happy.** |
| getting married | | since | happy | is | |

| keredo |

neutral connector

Keredo means **and**.

Examples

| Depāto | | ni | itta | keredo, | konde | imashita. |
| department store | | to | went | and | crowded | was |

/ **I went to the department store, and it was crowded.**

| Takushī | ni | notta | keredo, | takakatta desu. | / **I took a taxi, and it was expensive.** |
| taxi | on | got | and | was expensive | |

contrary reasoning

Here, *keredo* means **but**, **although**, **however**.

Examples

| Yonda | keredo, | wakarimasen deshita. | / **I read it, but I didn't understand it.** |
| read | but | didn't understand | |

| Eiga | wa | omoshirokatta | keredo, |
| movie | | was interesting | although |

| nete shimaimashita. | / **Although the movie was interesting, I fell asleep.** |
| fell asleep | |

nagara

simultaneous action

Nagara means **while** or **as**.

Examples

Aruki nagara, hanashimashita. / **While walking, we talked.**

walking while talked

Gohan o tabe nagara, terebi o mimasu. / **As I'm eating, I watch television.**

eating as TV watch

node

cause and effect

Node means **since** or **because** when followed by an "effect" clause.

Examples

Kumotte iru node, umi ni ikimasen. / **Since it's cloudy, I'm not going to the beach.**

cloudy is since beach to not going

Hashitta node, tsukaremashita. / **Because I ran, I got tired.**

ran because got tired

noni

contrast

Noni means **in spite of** or **although**, with strong contrast between the two clauses implied.

Examples

Tabetakunai   noni,   tabemashita. / **Although I didn't want to eat it, I ate it.**

didn't want to eat   **although**   **ate**

Takai   noni,   kaimashita. / **Although it was expensive, I bought it.**

expensive   **although**   **bought**

to

condition

When discussing under what condition, or under which circumstance, *to* means **if** or **when**.

Examples

Kangaeru to   wakarimasu. / **If you think, you'll understand it.**

think   **if**   **will understand**

Kuji ni iku to, Sano san ni   aemasu. / **If you go there at 9, you can see Mr. Sano.**

9 at go if   **can see**

Tōkyō ni tsuku   to,   ame ga futte imashita. / **When I arrived in Tokyo, it was raining.**

arrived when rain   falling was

§6.4 PARTICLES USED WITH SENTENCES

The following particles are used at the end of sentences.

ka	yo
ne	wa

ka

question marker

Ka is like the English question mark at the end of a sentence. In Japanese, however, the word order of a statement does not change when a question is formed.

Examples

Horiguchi san wa, kirei   desu. / **Mrs. Horiguchi is beautiful.**

beautiful is

Horiguchi san wa, kirei desu ka. / **Is Mrs. Horiguchi beautiful?**

is   ?

Imōto san wa, sensei desu ka. / **Is your sister a teacher?**

sister   teacher is   ?

Doko de ban gohan o tabetai desu ka. / **Where do you want to eat dinner?**

where   dinner   want to eat   ?

Itsu   eigo o benkyō shimashita ka. / **When did you study English?**

when English   studied   ?

ne

confirmation

Ne is similar to the English tag questions **don't you think
so**, or **isn't it?** It calls for the listener to agree with or confirm
what the speaker has said.

Examples

Atsui desu | ne. | / **It's hot, isn't it?**

is hot **isn't it**

Omoshiroi eiga deshita | ne. | / **It was an
interesting
movie, wasn't it?**

interesting movie was wasn't it

yo

emphatic

One usage of *yo* is similar to the English exclamation point.
In that sense, it conveys emotion or strong feeling. It can
also be an expression of emphasis, such as **I'm certain**
(of what has just been said). Because men and women use
yo differently, and because it can be assertive, beginners
should use it with care.

Examples

Benkyō shinasai | yo. / **Study!**

study

Fujisan wa, kirei desu yo. / **Mt. Fuji is beautiful!**

Mt. Fuji beautiful is !

wa

female sentence ending

Used by women, *wa* doesn't translate easily. It can have both an emphatic function and a softening effect.

Examples

Totemo atsui wa. / **It's very hot.**

very is hot

Watakushi ga suru wa. / **I'll do it.**

will do

- In kansai dialect, men use *wa* as an emphatic expression with different pitch from standard female usage.

§7.

Verbs

§7.1
WHAT ARE VERBS?

Verbs are words that describe an action, a process, or a state of being.

Verbs have different forms which enable you to express time, intention, feelings, politeness, etc. Japanese verbs express these things too, but in different ways from those of English and other Indo-European languages. As you have seen in §3, for example, the main verb of a Japanese sentence must be at the end. In this section, you will see other differences, as well as some similarities.

§7.2
AGREEMENT

In English a verb must agree with its subject in person and number. In the present tense, for example, a subject in the first person takes a different verb form from a subject in the third person. And a plural subject in the third person takes a different verb form from a singular subject.

Examples

Person	Singular	Plural
First Person	**I go**	**we go**
Second Person	**you go**	**you go**
Third Person	**he/she/it goes**	**they go**

• In Japanese, agreement is not an issue. Verbs do not have different forms to indicate person, number, or gender. The *same* verb form is used no matter what the subject. This is true for all tenses.

Examples

Person	Singular	Plural
First Person	ikimasu / **I go**	ikimasu / **we go**
Second Person	ikimasu / **you go**	ikimasu / **you go**
Third Person	ikimasu / **he/she/ it goes**	ikimasu / **they go**

- This principle is easy to understand if you remember the following: If the meaning is clear from the context in a Japanese sentence, a pronoun is not necessary. Therefore, *Ikimasu* is both a verb and a sentence.

- In English, except for the imperative, or command form, a sentence consisting of a verb alone is not possible.

§7.3 VERB CONJUGATIONS

Japanese verbs can be classified into two major groups, or conjugations. The only exceptions are two irregular verbs: *suru*, **to do**, and *kuru*, **to come**.

These groupings are a basic key to the Japanese verb system. They enable you to change the verb forms for different tenses and moods.

In a dictionary, an English verb is listed in its infinitive, or **to** form: **(to) go**, **(to) see**, etc. A Japanese verb, on the other hand, is listed in what is called its "dictionary form." The dictionary form is the basis for categorizing a verb into one of the two major conjugations.

The two groups differ in how they form their stems and their infinitives. The stem is the most important inflectional base, which may change, or to which different suffixes, or endings, are added, to show tense, mood, and politeness level. The infinitive is the second most important inflectional base.

§7.3–1 The Consonant Conjugation

In this group, the verb stems end in a consonant. Therefore, they may be called **c-stem** verbs, as we shall do here. Because the stems are formed by dropping the final **u**, this is also referred to as the **u-dropping conjugation**, and the verbs may be called **u-dropping verbs**.

How can you tell a Consonant Conjugation verb?

- If the dictionary form ends in anything but *-eru* or *-iru*, it belongs in this group.

How do you form the stem?

- To form the stem of the verb, drop the final *-u*.

Examples

DICTIONARY FORM	STEM	ENGLISH
isogu	isog-	**to hurry**
kaku	kak-	**to write**
nuru	nur-	**to paint**
tobu	tob-	**to fly**
shinu	shin-	**to die**
yomu	yom-	**to read**

- For a few verbs, certain sound changes are necessary:

  If a verb ends in *-su*, the stem ends in *sh* before a suffix beginning with *i*, or *s* before other suffixes.

  If a verb ends in *-tsu*, the stem ends in *ch* before a suffix beginning with *i*, or *t* before other suffixes. For example:

DICTIONARY FORM	STEM	ENGLISH
dasu	das- dash-	**to take out**
kasu	kas- kash-	**to lend**
matsu	mat- mach-	**to wait**
tatsu	tat- tach-	**to stand**

If a verb ends in *-au*, *-iu*, or *-ou*, it is still considered a c-stem verb, and it belongs in this group, even though a vowel remains after the *u* is dropped. The reason is that a missing "*w*" is considered the final consonant of the stem. That *w*, although not used in the affirmative forms, is needed for some of the negative forms. For example:

DICTIONARY FORM	STEM	ENGLISH
shimau	shima(w)-	**to put away**
kau	ka(w)-	**to buy**
iu	i(w)-	**to say**
omou	omo(w)-	**to think**

- Some verbs that end in -*eru* and -*iru* belong to the c-stem verb group. Here are a few examples:

DICTIONARY FORM	STEM	ENGLISH
hairu	hair-	**to enter**
kaeru	kaer-	**to return**
shiru	shir-	**to know**
kiru	kir-	**to cut**
iru	ir-	**to need**

Note that *kiru*, **to cut**, is a c-stem verb. When pronounced, the first syllable is stressed. The verb *kiru*, **to wear**, is a v-stem verb (see **§7.3–2**). When pronounced, the second syllable is stressed.

§7.3–2
The Vowel
Conjugation

In this group, the verb stems end in a vowel. Therefore, they may be called **v-stem** verbs, as we shall do here. Because the stems are formed by dropping the final **ru**, this is also referred to as the **ru-dropping conjugation**, and the verbs may be called **ru-dropping verbs**.

How can you tell a Vowel Conjugation verb?

- Most verbs with dictionary forms which end in -*eru* and -*iru* belong in this group. (For some exceptions, see **§7.3–1**.)

How do you form the stem?

- To form the stem of the verb, drop the final -*ru*.

Examples

DICTIONARY FORM	STEM	ENGLISH
ageru	age-	**to give, to raise**
dekiru	deki-	**to be able**
hajimeru	hajime-	**to begin**
iru	i-	**to be**
kangaeru	kangae-	**to think**
miru	mi-	**to see**
neru	ne-	**to sleep**
taberu	tabe-	**to eat**
kiru	ki-	**to wear**

§7.4
THE INFINITIVE

The infinitive is also an important base for constructing other verb forms. To form the infinitive, do the following:

- for c-stem verbs, add *-i* to the stem. For example:

DICTIONARY FORM	STEM	INFINITIVE
isogu	isog-	isogi-
kaku	kak-	kaki-
nuru	nur-	nuri-
tobu	tob-	tobi-
shinu	shin-	shini-
yomu	yom-	yomi-

- for v-stem verbs, add *nothing* to the stem. (In this conjugation, the stem and the infinitive are the same.) For example:

DICTIONARY FORM	STEM	INFINITIVE
ageru	age-	age-
dekiru	deki-	deki-
hajimeru	hajime-	hajime-
iru	i-	i-
kangaeru	kangae-	kangae-
miru	mi-	mi-

• For the irregular verbs, the forms are as follows:

DICTIONARY FORM	INFINITIVE
kuru	ki-
suru	shi-

§7.5 PLAIN AND POLITE FORMS

The Japanese use different sets, or levels, of verb forms, depending on the politeness requirements of the situation, and the relationship among the speakers. For non-Japanese using the different politeness levels correctly takes a great deal of experience with the Japanese language and culture.

The two most common levels are called *plain* and *polite*. The plain verb forms are used with immediate family members and close friends and associates. The polite forms have a wider range, and are more appropriate for general use, especially for students of Japanese.

The examples below show two ways of saying the same thing, one plain style, and one polite style. Note the different verb forms.

Plain	Present	da / dictionary form
	Past	datta / -ta, -da
Polite	Present	desu / -masu
	Past	deshita / -mashita

• Both plain and polite forms are introduced with new verbs throughout this chapter.

Examples

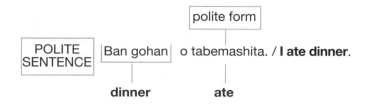

Although readers of this book should use the polite level, both forms must be learned. This is because the plain form can function other than as the main verb. When the main verb of the sentence, the one at the end, is in the polite form, other verbs earlier in the same sentence usually take the plain form.

The following examples show two sentences that say the same thing, one plain style, the other polite. Note that both sentences use a plain verb form, *tabeta*, for **ate**. And keep in mind that the verb at the end determines the politeness level for the entire sentence.

Examples

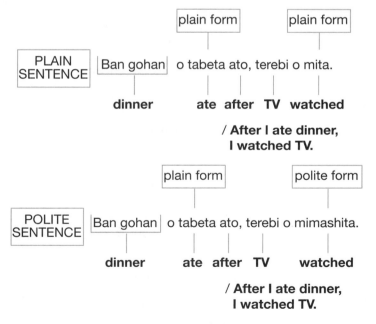

In the sections on verbs that follow, both the plain and polite forms will be given. Although there are other, more formal verb forms, these two levels should be appropriate for the reader's needs.

§7.6
THE "TO BE"
VERBS

English has one verb to express the meaning **to be**, although that verb takes several forms (**am**, **is**, **are**, **was**, **were**, etc.). Japanese has three different words, each expressing a particular aspect of the meaning of **to be**: *desu*, *arimasu*, and *imasu*.

> *desu*

Often called the copula, *desu* is used when you want to indicate such things as condition, quality, number, characteristics, or identity. You can understand it more easily if you think of *desu* as meaning not only **is**, but also **equals**, especially with two nouns or noun phrases. If you can substitute **equals** for **is** in an English sentence such as **This equals/is a book** or **Mrs**. **Smith equals/is my best friend**, *desu* is the word you want.

Although the polite forms *desu* (present) and *deshita* (past) are the ones you will use most often, you should know the following forms as well.

desu / **is, equals**		**Affirmative**	**Negative**
Present	Plain	da	dewa nai
	Polite	desu	dewa arimasen
Past	Plain	datta	dewa nakatta
	Polite	deshita	dewa arimasen deshita
Probable	Plain	darō	dewa nai darō
	Polite	deshō	dewa nai deshō

• For informal or familiar usage, *ja* can replace *dewa*.

Examples

Kore wa, hon desu. / **This is a book.**

   | | |

   this   **book** **is**

Tanaka san wa, sensei desu. / **Mr. Tanaka is a teacher.**

         |

      teacher

Otenki ga, ii desu. / **The weather is good.**

weather good

Otenki ga, warui deshō. / **The weather will probably be bad.**

bad will probably be

Ano hito wa, kinō byōki deshita. / **He was sick yesterday.**

he yesterday sick was

---

arimasu

Arimasu means **is** or **exists** for the location of inanimate things. It also expresses the idea of English **to have**. If you think of the meaning as **(something) exists/is located (somewhere)**, *arimasu* is the word you want. Because *arimasu* is a stative (non-action) verb, the particle *ni* is used with expressions of location.

Example

Hon wa, tēburu no ue ni arimasu. / **The book is on the table.**

table 's top on

In the **to have** meaning of *arimasu*, the thing possessed is the subject of the sentence, and takes the particle *ga*.

Examples

Okane ga arimasu ka. / **Do you have any money? (As for you, does money exist?)**

money is

Hai, arimasu. / **Yes, I do. (Yes, it exists.)**

yes

Here are the other forms of arimasu:

arimasu / **is, exists**		**Affirmative**	**Negative**
Present	Plain	aru	nai
	Polite	arimasu	arimasen
Past	Plain	atta	nakatta
	Polite	arimashita	arimasen deshita
Probable	Plain	aru darō	nai darō
	Polite	aru deshō	nai deshō

Examples

Fujisan wa, Nihon ni arimasu. / **Mt. Fuji is in Japan.**

　　　　　　　　　　|　　|

　　　　　　　　　　in　　is

Ginza ni, sūpā ga arimasu ka. / **Is there a supermarket in Ginza?**

　　　　　　|

　　supermarket

Eki wa, doko ni arimasu ka. / **Where is the station?**

　　|　　　　|

station where

Jisho ga arimasu ka. / **Do you have a dictionary?**

　　|

dictionary

Iie, arimasen. / **No, I don't (have a dictionary).**

Koko ni kōen ga arimashita. / **There was a park here.**

　　|　　　　|　　　　|

here　 park　　 was

imasu

Imasu is also a stative (non-action) verb used to express **is** or **exists** for location. But *imasu* is used for living things—people, animals, insects (*not* plants). The particle *ni* is used with *imasu* when the location is specified.

Imasu is also used as an auxiliary verb to form the progressive tenses, where it functions just like the English **is**: **He is going, I was going,** etc. Because this meaning of *imasu* is discussed in **§7.7–4** and **§7.7–5**, the examples below will deal with only the locational meaning. First, here are the other forms of *imasu*:

imasu / **is, exists**		**Affirmative**	**Negative**
Present	Plain	iru	inai
	Polite	imasu	imasen
Past	Plain	ita	inakatta
	Polite	imashita	imasen deshita
Probable	Plain	iru darō	inai darō
	Polite	iru deshō	inai deshō

Examples

Tanaka san wa imasu ka. / **Is Mr. Tanaka here?**

Hai, imasu. / **Yes, he is.**

Kinō Tōkyō ni imashita ka. / **Were you in Tokyo yesterday?**

yesterday   **were**

Neko wa doko ni imasu ka. / **Where is the cat?**

cat   **where**

Merī san wa, | raigetsu | Nihon ni

next month

| iru deshō. | / **Mary will probably be in Japan next month.**

will probably be

§7.7 THE INDICATIVE MOOD

The indicative mood allows you to express ordinary, objective statements, questions, etc. Tense refers to the time of the action or state expressed by the verb.

Sometimes Japanese is described as having just two tenses: the past and the non-past. At first, this sounds strange; on second thought, it can be a useful concept. What does it mean? It means that *Japanese does not have a separate future tense*. The past is the past, the non-past is everything else—that is, present and future. Here we will use more conventional terms (present and past), however.

Keep in mind as you look at the different tenses and moods that Japanese verbs do not change their form for gender and number.

§7.7–1 Present Tense

The present tense meanings in Japanese are similar to those of English: incomplete or habitual actions or states. The present tense is used for future time as well; Japanese has no separate future tense.

The plain form of the present tense is the same as the dictionary form, the one from which the stem is derived. The dictionary form was discussed in **§7.3**, Verb Conjugations.

plain form, c-stem verbs (see §7.3–1)

iku / **I go, you go, he/she/it goes, we go, they go, I will go, you will go, he/she/it will go, we will go, they will go**

yomu / **I read, you read, he/she/it reads, we read, they read, I will read, you will read, he/she/it will read, we will read, they will read**

plain form, v-stem verbs (see §7.3–1)

miru / **I see, you see, he/she/it sees, we see, they see, I will see, you will see, he/she/it will see, we will see, they will see**

taberu / **I eat, you eat, he/she/it eats, we eat, they eat, I will eat, you will eat, he/she/it will eat, we will eat, they will eat**

- To form the negative of the plain form, do the following:

c-stem verbs: add -*anai* to the stem.

| iku / ikanai | **go / don't go** |
| yomu / yomanai | **read / don't read** |

- Note that for c-stem verbs ending in -*au*, -*iu*, or -*ou*, you must add a *w* to the stem before adding -*anai* (see **§7.3–1**).

shimau / shimawanai	**put away / don't put away**
kau / kawanai	**buy / don't buy**
iu / iwanai	**say / don't say**
omou / omowanai	**think / don't think**

v-stem verbs: add -*nai* to the stem

hajimeru / hajimenai	**begin / don't begin**
kangaeru / kangaenai	**think / don't think**
taberu / tabenai	**eat / don't eat**
ageru / agenai	**give / don't give**
miru / minai	**see / don't see**

- The polite present is sometimes referred to as the *masu* form. It can be constructed in two different ways.

Either: | Add -*masu* to the infinitive. (See **§7.4**.) |
|---|

c-stem verbs	isogi + masu	isogimasu / **hurry**
	kaki + masu	kakimasu / **write**
	nuri + masu	nurimasu / **paint**
	tobi + masu	tobimasu / **fly**
	shini + masu	shinimasu / **die**
	yomi + masu	yomimasu / **read**
v-stem verbs	age + masu	agemasu / **give**
	hajime + masu	hajimemasu / **begin**
	kangae + masu	kangaemasu / **think about**
	mi + masu	mimasu / **see**
	ki + masu	kimasu / **wear**
	ori + masu	orimasu / **get off**

Or: | For c-stem verbs, add *-imasu* to the stem.

isogu isog + imasu	isogimasu / **hurry**
kaku kak + imasu	kakimasu / **write**
nuru nur + imasu	nurimasu / **paint**

For v-stem verbs, add *-masu* to the stem.

hajimeru hajime + masu	hajimemasu / **begin**
kangaeru kangae + masu	kangaemasu / **think about**
miru mi + masu	mimasu / **see**

• To form the polite negative, do the following:

For all verbs, simply change the ending from *masu* to *masen*.

ikimasu / ikimasen	**go / don't go**
wakarimasu / wakarimasen	**understand /**
	don't understand
kakimasu / kakimasen	**write / don't write**
mimasu / mimasen	**see / don't see**
oshiemasu / oshiemasen	**teach / don't teach**

Here are a few verbs in their present tense conjugations:

Verb			**Affirmative**	**Negative**
taberu / **eat**				
Present	Plain		taberu	tabenai
	Polite		tabemasu	tabemasen
nomu / **drink**				
Present	Plain		nomu	nomanai
	Polite		nomimasu	nomimasen
suru / **do**				
Present	Plain		suru	shinai
	Polite		shimasu	shimasen

And some present tense sentences:

Examples

Watakushi wa, kōhī o |nomimasen.| / **I don't drink**
           | | **coffee.**
       coffee don't drink

Tanaka san wa, mainichi sushi o tabemasu. / **Mr. Tanaka**
            | | **eats sushi**
                        every day.
     every day   eat

|Ano hitotachi| wa, terebi o mimasen. / **They don't**
    | | | **watch**
                          television.
   they   television don't watch

Nihongo ga wakarimasu ka. / **Do you understand**
               | **Japanese?**
       understand

Ashita   Kyōto ni   ikimasu. / **I'll go to Kyoto tomorrow.**
  | |
.tomorrow   will go

§7.7–2
Past Tense

Like English, the past tense is used for actions completed in the past (**I ate, I studied**, etc.). It is also used to express the equivalent of the English present perfect (**I have walked, I have eaten**, etc.).

Forming the plain past tense is easy for v-stem verbs, more complex for c-stem verbs.

> For plain form, v-stem verbs: add -*ta* to the stem.

taberu / tabeta	**eat / ate**
oshieru / oshieta	**teach / taught**
miru / mita	**see / saw**
ageru / ageta	**give / gave**

For plain form, c-stem verbs: do the following:

- Look at the *final* syllable in the plain present form (dictionary form) of the verb. Find the syllable in column A below. Change it to the syllable(s) in column B.

	A	B
	change this ⟶ to this	
omou	u ⟶ tta	omotta / **thought**
motsu	tsu ⟶ tta	motta / **held**
nuru	ru ⟶ tta	nutta / **painted**
nomu	mu ⟶ nda	nonda / **drank**
shinu	nu ⟶ nda	shinda / **died**
tobu	bu ⟶ nda	tonda / **flew**
kiku	ku ⟶ ita	kiita / **asked**
oyogu	gu ⟶ ida	oyoida / **swam**
hanasu	su ⟶ shita	hanashita / **talked**

- To form the negative of the plain past tense, do the following:

c-stem verbs: add *-anakatta* to the stem

iku	itta / ikanakatta	**went / didn't go**
yomu	yonda / yomanakatta	**read / didn't read**
kau(w)	katta / kawanakatta	**bought / didn't buy**
isogu	isoida / isoganakatta	**hurried / didn't hurry**

v-stem verbs: add *-nakatta* to the stem.

hajimeru	hajimeta / hajimenakatta	**began / didn't begin**
taberu	tabeta / tabenakatta	**ate / didn't eat**
ageru	ageta / agenakatta	**gave / didn't give**
miru	mita / minakatta	**saw / didn't see**

> For the polite past tense, change the present tense ending from *masu* to *mashita*.

ikimasu / ikimashita	**go / went**
mimasu / mimashita	**see / saw**
kaimasu / kaimashita	**buy / bought**
wakarimasu / wakarimashita	**understand / understood**
tabemasu / tabemashita	**eat / ate**
shimasu / shimashita	**do / did**
kimasu / kimashita	**come / came**

- For the negative of the polite past, add the word *deshita* to the polite present negative.

tabemasen / tabemasen deshita	**don't eat / didn't eat**
ikimasen / ikimasen deshita	**don't go / didn't go**
hashirimasen / hashirimasen deshita	**don't run / didn't run**
kaimasen / kaimasen deshita	**don't buy / didn't buy**

Here are a few verbs in their past tense conjugations:

Verb		Affirmative	Negative
kiru / **to put on (clothes)**			
Past	Plain	kita	kinakatta
	Polite	kimashita	kimasen deshita
yomu / **to read**			
Past	Plain	yonda	yomanakatta
	Polite	yomimashita	yomimasen deshita
suru / **to do**			
Past	Plain	shita	shinakatta
	Polite	shimashita	shimasen deshita

And some past tense sentences:

Examples

Itsu kimashita ka. / **When did you come?**

when   came

Kinō shimasen deshita. / **I didn't do it yesterday.**

yesterday   **didn't do**

Owarimashita. / **It's finished.**

finished

Doko de kaimashita ka. / **Where did you buy it?**

bought

Naze ikimasen deshita ka. / **Why didn't you go?**

why   **didn't go**

§7.7–3
The Gerund

Often referred to as the "*-te* form," the gerund is a useful form of the Japanese verb. Alone, it does not have tense or mood. But it combines with other verb forms to create tenses and moods, such as the continuous tenses and the imperative mood, for example. It has other uses as well.

One caution: The term "gerund" may be misleading. In English, a gerund is the **-ing** form of a verb when functioning as a noun (**I like swimming, Reading is my favorite hobby**, etc. For this use, see **§7.19**). The Japanese gerund is a verb form, *not* a noun. Indeed, in the progressive tenses, it functions much like the English **-ing** form.

Gerunds are regular in form and easy to construct.

Start with the plain past tense (see **§7.7–2**), and change the final *-a* to *-e*.

Present	Past	Gerund
aruku / **walk**	aruita	aruite
kiku / **ask, listen**	kiita	kiite
taberu / **eat**	tabeta	tabete
hanasu / **speak**	hanashita	hanashite
yomu / **read**	yonda	yonde

Note that for the copula, *desu*, the plain past tense is *datta* and the gerund is *de*.

One important use of the gerund is when listing actions in a neutral sequence (with no strong contrast or emphasis) within a sentence. All but the last verb are gerunds.

Example

Sūpā ni   itte,   niku o katte, uchi ni

went   meat   bought

kaerimashita. / **I went to the supermarket, bought some meat, and returned home.**

returned

**§7.7–4
Present
Progressive**

Japanese uses the present progressive for action in progress or continuous action, state of being, and also to express the meaning of the English present perfect.

Unlike English, it cannot be used to express future meaning (**Tomorrow he's going to New York**, or **I'm getting my degree next year**, etc.).

To form the present progressive, start with the gerund, and add the appropriate form of the verb *iru*. The plain form is used in informal conversation, of course. The polite form, appropriate for general use, is given here. Note that *iru* when used alone as a verb can only refer to living things. With the gerund, it is used for inanimate things as well.

Affirmative	Negative
aruite imasu / **walking**	aruite imasen / **not walking**
kiite imasu / **listening**	kiite imasen / **not listening**
tabete imasu / **eating**	tabete imasen / **not eating**
hanashite imasu / **speaking**	hanashite imasen / **not speaking**
yonde imasu / **reading**	yonde imasen / **not reading**
nonde imasu / **drinking**	nonde imasen / **not drinking**
motte imasu / **holding**	motte imasen / **not holding**
oyoide imasu / **swimming**	oyoide imasen / **not swimming**

When the meaning of this tense is an action in progress, the verb is often transitive (a verb that takes an object). This is similar to the English present progressive.

Examples

Ima, ban gohan o tabete imasu. / **I'm eating dinner now.**

now   **am eating**

Nani o shite imasu ka. / **What are you doing?**

what   **are doing**

Eigo o benkyō shite imasu. / **I'm studying English.**

am studying

Tegami o |kaite imasu.| / **I'm writing a letter.**

letter   am writing

When the meaning is a state of being, the verb is often intransitive (a verb that doesn't take an object). This is not like an English progressive tense usage; the explanations after the examples below should help clarify the meanings.

Examples

Mado ga |aite imasu.|/ **The window is open. (Someone opened it, and it's still open.)**

window   is open

Mise ga |shimatte imasu.| / **The store is closed. (Someone closed it, and it's still closed.)**

store   is closed

|Ano hito |wa |futotte imasu.| / **He is fat. (He got fat, and he's still fat.)**

he   is fat

Haha wa Tōkyō ni |itte imasu.| / **Mother is in Tokyo. (She went to Tokyo, and she's still there.)**

mother   is

Tsukarete imasu. / **I'm tired. (I got tired, and I'm still tired.)**

tired

The present progressive can express the English present perfect tense—an action that began in the past and continues through the present. In the following sentences, notice how the time element, **for five years**, results in a present perfect meaning. Without it, the meaning is simply continuous action.

Examples

Kyōto ni gonen   kan | sunde imasu. | / **I have been living in Kyoto for five years.**

     five years   **for**   **am living**

Kyōto ni sunde imasu. / **I'm living in Kyoto.**

§7.7–5 Past Progressive

The past progressive is used for past continuous action or state of being.

The form is easy: start with the gerund, and change *imasu* to the past form: *imashita*. The negative is the gerund plus the negative past of *imashita*, which is *imasen deshita*.

Affirmative	Negative
aruite imashita / **was walking**	aruite imasen deshita / **wasn't walking**
kiite imashita / **was listening**	kiite imasen deshita / **wasn't listening**
tabete imashita / **was eating**	tabete imasen deshita / **wasn't eating**
hanashite imashita / **was speaking /**	hanashite imasen deshita / **wasn't speaking**
yonde imashita / **was reading**	yonde imasen deshita / **wasn't reading**
nonde imashita / **was drinking**	nonde imasen deshita / **wasn't drinking**
motte imashita / **was holding**	motte imasen deshita / **wasn't holding**
oyoide imashita / **was swimming**	oyoide imasen deshita / **wasn't swimming**

Here are some examples of past continuous action.

Examples

Haha wa, ban gohan o | tsukutte imashita. | / **Mother was preparing dinner.**

was making

Chichi wa, | hataraite imasen deshita. | / **Father wasn't working.**

father   **wasn't working**

Kyonen Nihongo o | benkyō shite imashita. | / **Last year I was studying Japanese.**

last year   **was studying**

Neko ga, | isu no | ue de | nete imashita. | / **The cat was sleeping on the chair.**

cat   **chair's top**   **was sleeping**

The following examples show past states of being.

Examples

Denki ga | tsuite imashita. | / **The light was on.**

light   **was on**

Doa ga | aite imashita. | / **The door was open.**

door   **was open**

Ano hito wa | yasete imashita. | / **She was thin.**

was thin

Tsukarete imasen deshita. / **I wasn't tired.**

tired

§7.8 THE PRESUMPTIVE MOOD

Sometimes called the "probable" mood, this has no exact equivalent in English, although it is important in Japanese. It enables speakers to use a verb form that can express *probability*, *belief*, or *intention* without being too direct. This mood has two sets of forms, one indicating probability, the second indicating intention.

darō, deshō form

This form expresses the speaker's belief that something will probably happen. It is easily constructed by adding *darō* or *deshō* (plain and polite, respectively) to the plain, or dictionary form, of the verb. This works for the negative of the plain form as well, and also for the past forms.

Present	
Plain	**Polite**
kuru darō	kuru deshō / **will probably come**
iku darō	iku deshō / **will probably go**
taberu darō	taberu deshō / **will probably eat**
Negative	
konai darō	konai deshō / **will probably not come**
ikanai darō	ikanai deshō / **will probably not go**
tabenai darō	tabenai deshō / **will probably not eat**
Past	
kita darō	kita deshō / **probably came**
itta darō	itta deshō / **probably went**
tabeta darō	tabeta deshō / **probably ate**
Negative	
konakatta darō	konakatta deshō / **probably didn't come**
ikanakatta darō	ikanakatta deshō / **probably didn't go**
tabanakatta darō	tabenakatta deshō / **probably didn't eat**

The examples below show some expanded dimensions of these forms, which can also be translated as **suppose**, **wonder**, **guess**, etc.

Examples

Ano hito wa, Nihon ni | iku deshō. | / **He'll probably go to Japan.**

will probably go

Konban   yuki   ga | furu darō. | / **Tonight it will probably snow.**

tonight   snow   will probably fall

Merī san wa, Nihon de   Nihongo o

Japan in Japanese

| hanashita deshō ka. | / **I wonder if Mary spoke Japanese in Japan.**

wonder if spoke

Jon san wa, | tsukareta deshō. | / **I suppose John got tired.**

suppose got tired

Yūbin wa, jūji ni | kuru deshō. | / **I guess the mail will come at 10.**

mail   10 at guess will come

-ō, -yō / -mashō forms

These differ somewhat in the plain and polite forms.

First consider the plain form, *-ō, -yō*. As a final verb at the end of a sentence, it expresses the speaker's intention. Considered abrupt, it is used mostly by men. It can also mean "Let's (do something)," but for this, the *-mashō* form is preferred. As a medial verb (not at the end of the sentence), it expresses intention or probability. The forms are made as follows:

- For c-stem verbs, start with the plain, or dictionary form, and change the final -*u* to -*ō*.

Present	Presumptive
nuru / **paint**	nurō / **will probably paint, will/let's paint**
kiku / **ask**	kikō / **will probably ask, will/let's ask**

- For v-stem verbs, start with the stem, and add -*yō*.

Present	Stem	Presumptive
taberu / **eat**	tabe-	tabeyō / **will probably eat, will/let's eat**
miru / **see**	mi-	miyō / **will probably see, will/let's see**

- The irregular verb forms are as follows:

suru / **do**	shiyō / **will probably do, will/let's do**
kuru / **come**	koyō / **will probably come, will/let's come**

- The negative forms, infrequently used, are not needed here.
- Note how the *ō* and *yō* forms are used in medial and final position, and the differences in meaning.

Examples

Konban hayaku   neyō

tonight   early   probably go to sleep

    to   omoimasu. / **I think I'll probably go to sleep
                        early tonight.**

    that   think

Watakushi ga ikō. / **I will go.**

will go

Tabeyō. / **Let's eat.**

Now look at the polite form, -*mashō*. This can express several things: the speaker's intention to do something, a polite description of the probability of someone else's doing something, or, most common, the idea of "Let's" or "Shall we?"

To construct this form, add -*mashō* to the infinitive of the verb.

Plain	Infinitive	-*mashō* Form
yomu / **read**	yomi-	yomimashō / **let's read**
miru / **see**	mi-	mimashō / **let's see**
taberu / **eat**	tabe-	tabemashō / **let's eat**
iku / **go**	iki-	ikimashō / **let's go**

Here are some examples of some common uses of this form:

Examples

Ginza ni ikimashō. / **Let's go to Ginza.**

let's go

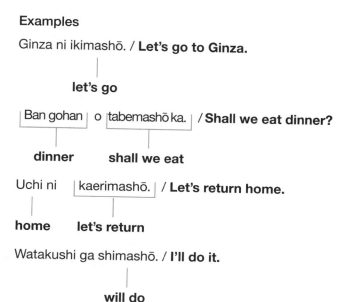

Ban gohan o tabemashō ka. / **Shall we eat dinner?**

dinner   shall we eat

Uchi ni kaerimashō. / **Let's return home.**

home   let's return

Watakushi ga shimashō. / **I'll do it.**

will do

Jon san ga kimashō. / **John will probably come.**

| will probably come

- Note that the last sentence above would mean the same thing using the *deshō* form. For example:

Jon san ga |kuru deshō.| / **John will probably come.**

will probably come.

§7.9 THE IMPERATIVE MOOD

The true imperative or command form in Japanese is too abrupt for most usage. However, you should recognize it.

The imperative is formed by adding *-e* to the stem of c-stem verbs, and *-ro* to the stem of v-stem verbs. To form the negative imperatives, add *-na* to the plain present form of the verb.

Plain	Imperative	Imperative (Negative)
iku / **go**	ike / **go!**	ikuna / **don't go!**
kiku / **listen**	kike / **listen!**	kikuna / **don't listen!**
taberu / **eat**	tabero / **eat!**	taberuna / **don't eat!**
miru / **look**	miro / **look!**	miruna / **don't look!**

A somewhat less harsh form is made by adding *-nasai* to the infinitive form of the verb. This is not used with negative forms.

iku / **go**	ikinasai / **go**
taberu / **eat**	tabenasai / **eat**

Examples

Yukkuri hanashinasai. / **Speak slowly.**

| |

slowly   speak

Koko ni kinasai. / **Come here.**

here come

The form of the imperative commonly used for polite requests or commands is the gerund, or -*te* form, with the word *kudasai*.

kuru / **come**	Kite kudasai. / **Please come.**
taberu / **eat**	Tabete kudasai. / **Please eat.**
suwaru / **sit down**	Suwatte kudasai. / **Please sit down.**
kiku / **listen**	Kiite kudasai. / **Please listen.**
hanasu / **speak**	Hanashite kudasai. / **Please speak.**

Examples

Ryokō ni tsuite | hanashite kudasai. | / **Please tell me about your trip.**

trip   about   please tell

Tegami o | dashite kudasai. | / **Please mail the letter.**

letter   please mail

Takushī o | yonde kudasai. | / **Please call a taxi.**

taxi   please call

For the negative of this structure, add -*de kudasai* to the negative of the plain present form.

Ikanaide kudasai. / **Please don't go.**
Shinpai shinaide kudasai. / **Please don't worry.**

Kudasai can also be used when requesting an object. In this usage another verb form is not needed.

Examples

Hon o   kudasai. / **Please give me a book.**

book please give

Kōhī o   kudasai. / **Please give me some coffee.**

coffee   please give

§7.10 THE CONDITIONAL MOOD

In Japanese, there are several ways of conveying the conditional, or "if" meaning. Although they can, in many cases, be used interchangeably, there are slight differences in meaning.

> *-eba* form

This is sometimes called the "provisional" form, because it means "if" in the sense of "provided something happens (now or in the future)." In the negative form, it can mean "unless."

For the *-eba* form, drop the final *-u* of the dictionary form of the verb and add *-eba*. For the negative, drop the final *-i* of the plain negative form and add *-kereba*.

Plain	Conditional
kuru / **come**	kureba / **if, provided I (you, etc.) come** konakereba / **if I don't come, unless I come**
miru / **see**	mireba / **if, provided I see** minakereba / **if I don't see, unless I see**
yomu / **read**	yomeba / **if, provided I read** yomanakereba / **if I don't read, unless I read**
taberu / **eat**	tabereba / **if, provided I eat** tabenakereba / **if I don't eat, unless I eat**

Examples

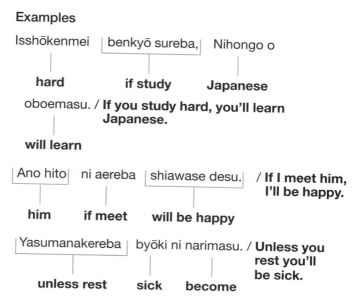

With verbal adjectives (-*i* adjectives), drop the -*i* and add *kereba*. For the negative, use the adverbial form (yasuku) [see §8.2–3] and add *nakereba*. For example:

Adjective	Conditional
yasui / **cheap**	yasukereba / **if it's cheap, if it were cheap**
	yasukunakereba / **if it's not cheap, unless it's cheap**

Examples

Omoshirokereba, yomimasu. / **If it's interesting, I'll read it.**

if interesting   read

-*tara* form

The -*tara* form can express a wide range of conditional "when" and "if" meaning: past occurrence, hypothetical conditions in the past, future or habitual action. (See the forms below.)

To construct the -*tara* form, start with the plain past verb form and add -*ra*.

tabetara / **if I (you,** *etc.*) **should eat (it)**

if I (you, *etc.*) **were to eat (it)**

when I (you, *etc.*) **eat (it)**

when I (you, *etc.*) **ate (it)**

For the negative, do the same: tabenakattara / **If I (you, etc.) didn't eat (it).**

Examples

Honya ni   ittara, shimatte imashita. / **When I went to the bookstore, it was closed.**

bookstore when went was closed

Benkyō shitara, wakatta deshō. / **If I had studied, I would have understood.**

if had studied   understood

Kōhī o nondara, neraremasen. / **When I drink coffee, I can't sleep.**

coffee when drink can't sleep

Notice the use of -*tara* forms with -*i* and -*na* adjectives and with nouns.

Examples

| Takakattara | kaimasen. | / **If it's expensive, I won't buy it.** |
| if it is expensive | won't buy | |

Soko ga | shizuka dattara | ikimasu. / **If it were quiet there, I would go.**

there   if it were quiet   would go

Ii hon | dattara, | kaimasu. / **If it were a good book, I would buy it.**

good   if it were   would buy

Other useful conditional forms are *nara* and *to*.

$$\boxed{nara}$$

with verbs	Present: iku nara / **if I (you, etc.) go** Past: itta nara / **if I had gone**
with verbal adjectives	Present: ōkii nara / **if it is / were big** Past: ōkikatta nara / **if it had been big**
with adjectival nouns	Present: kirei nara / **if it is / were pretty** Past: kirei datta nara / **if it had been pretty**
with nouns	gakusei nara / **if I am / were a student**

Similar to the *-tara* forms in meaning, *nara* can be used for **if** and **after**. In some uses, it has a strong contrary-to-fact element, like the subjunctive mood of English.

Examples

Watakushi ga   kanemochi nara   yotto o

rich person   if   sailboat

kaimasu. / **If I were rich, I would buy a sailboat.**

would buy

Isogu nara, chikatetsu de ikinasai. / **If you're in a hurry, take a subway.**

hurry   if   subway   take

to

To is used with the present forms of verbs and verbal adjectives, adjectival nouns, and with nouns. In many cases, the meaning is the same as that of the *-tara* or *-eba* forms.

Examples

Sake o nomu   to,   nemuku narimasu. / **Whenever I drink sake, I become sleepy.**

drink whenever sleepy become

Tenki ga ii   to,   kōen ni ikimasu. / **When/if the weather is good, I go/will go to the park.**

weather good when/if park   go

§7.11 THE POTENTIAL MOOD

To express the idea of capability or possibility (**can** or **be able to** in English), add *-eru* (plain) or *-emasu* (polite) to the stem of c-stem verbs, and *-rareru* (plain) or *-raremasu* (polite) to the stem of v-stem verbs. The negatives are formed regularly: Add *-enai* / *-emasen* to the stem of c-stem verbs, and *-rarenai* / *-raremasen* to the stem of v-stem verbs.

Examples

Merī san wa, Nihongo ga hanasemasu. / **Mary can speak Japanese.**

Japanese   can speak

Nanji ni   aemasu ka. / **What time can I see you?**

what time can see

Kyō   ikenai nara, ashita |ikemasu| ka. / **If you can't go today, can you go tomorrow?**

today can't go if tomorrow can go   ?

Another way to express the potential is as follows:

- Place the appropriate form of the verb *dekiru* / **can do** after a noun (plus the particle *ga*).

Examples

Nihongo ga dekimasu. / **I can speak Japanese.**

Japanese   can do

Tenisu ga dekimasu. / **I can play tennis.**

tennis   can do

Ryōri ga dekimasen. / **I can't cook.**

cooking   can't do

A verb form can be used with this structure as well, but it must first be nominalized, or made into a noun form. To nominalize a verb, do the following:

- Add the word *koto* to the plain, or dictionary form, of the verb. Then it can be used with *ga* and *dekiru* / *dekimasu*.

Examples

Nihongo o yomu koto ga dekimasu. / **I can read Japanese.**

Japanese read   can do

Merī san wa, oyogu koto ga dekimasen. / **Mary can't swim.**

swim   can't do

Kinō, Tanaka san ni au koto ga dekimashita.

yesterday   **see**   **could do**

/ **Yesterday, I could see Ms. Tanaka.**

§7.12 THE PASSIVE VOICE

Japanese has two ways of using the passive. The first is with transitive verbs, as in English. In such sentences, the "doer" may or may not be expressed. (**My wallet was stolen**, *or* **My wallet was stolen by a pickpocket**.)

- To form the passive, add *-areru*, *-aremasu* to the stems of c-stem verbs, and *-rareru*, *-raremasu* to the stems of v-stem verbs. For the negative, add *-arenai*, *-aremasen* to the stems of c-stem verbs, and *-rarenai*, *-raremasen* to the stems of v-stem verbs.

> nusumu / **steal**, nusumareru, nusumaremasu / **is stolen**
> oikakeru / **chase**, oikakerareru, oikakeraremasu /
>   **is chased**

Examples

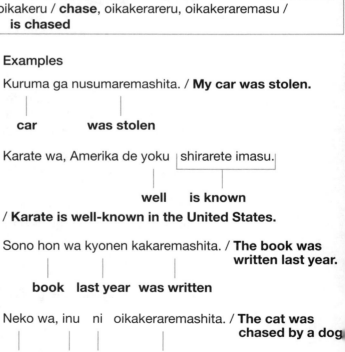

Kuruma ga nusumaremashita. / **My car was stolen.**

car   **was stolen**

Karate wa, Amerika de yoku | shirarete imasu.|

                         well   **is known**

/ **Karate is well-known in the United States.**

Sono hon wa kyonen kakaremashita. / **The book was written last year.**

book   last year   was written

Neko wa, inu   ni   oikakeraremashita. / **The cat was chased by a dog**

cat   dog   by   was chased

So | mirarete imasu. | / **It is seen that way.**

that way   **it is seen**

- Note that the use of this type of passive is more limited in Japanese than in English. While passive forms are grammatically possible for many verbs, the resulting sentences may be awkward.

The second way of using the passive in Japanese, for which English has no corresponding use, may be called the "adversity" passive. You can think of it as the "too bad" or "regrettably" passive. This means that something happened to someone and it had an adverse effect on that person. The verb may be transitive or intransitive. Because this is quite unlike English, read the following sentences carefully, especially the translations.

- Note the use of *ni* in the passive sentences below.

Examples

Active
Merī san no okāsan ga shinimashita. / **Mary's mother died.**

Mary   **'s mother**   **died**

Passive
Merī san wa okāsan   ni | shinaremashita. | / **Mary's mother died (on her). (Lit: Mary was died by her mother.)**

Mary   **mother**   **by**   **was died**

Active
Ame ga furimashita. / **It rained. (The rain fell.)**

rain   **fell**

Passive
Tanaka san wa ame ni furaremashita. / **Mr. Tanaka was caught in the rain. (Lit: Mr. Tanaka was fallen by rain.)**

rain by was fallen

§7.13 THE CAUSATIVE

The causative forms in Japanese express the idea of making or causing someone to do something: **I made my brother clean his room.** It also can mean **let** or **allow**: **Please let me go.**

- To form the causative, add -*aseru*, -*asemasu* to the stem of c-stem verbs (-*asenai*, -*asemasen* for the negative), and add -*saseru, -sasemasu* to the stem of v-stem verbs (-*sasenai*, -*sasemasen* for the negative).

---

yomu / **read**, yomaseru, yomasemasu /
       make (someone) read, let (someone) read

taberu / **eat**, tabesaseru, tabesasemasu /
       make (someone) eat, let (someone) eat

Examples

Merī san o mise ni ikasemashita. / **I made Mary go to the store.**
       store to   made go

Okāsan wa, kodomo o nekasemashita. / **The mother made the child go to bed.**
  mother   child   made sleep

Watakushi ni harawasete kudasai. / **Please let me pay.**
      let pay   please

Otōto ni | benkyō sasemashita. | / **I made my younger brother study.**
  younger   made study
  brother

§7.14 THE CAUSATIVE PASSIVE

The causative passive form expresses the idea that the subject of the sentence is made to do something in the sense of being forced.

- To form the causative passive, add -*aserareru*, -*aseraremasu* to the stem of c-stem verbs (-*aserarenai*, -*aseraremasen* for the negative), and add -*saserareru*, -*saseraremasu* to the stem of v-stem verbs (-*saserarenai*, -*saseraremasen* for the negative).

iku / **go**	ikaserareru, ikaseraremasu / **be made to go**
taberu / **eat**	tabesaserareru, tabesaseraremasu / **be made to eat**

Examples

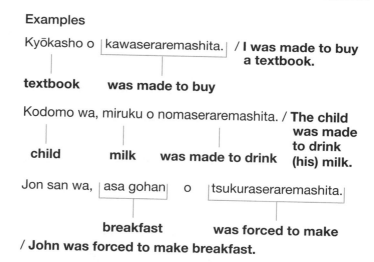

Kyōkasho o | kawaseraremashita. | / **I was made to buy a textbook.**

textbook　　**was made to buy**

Kodomo wa, miruku o nomaseraremashita. / **The child was made to drink (his) milk.**

child　　**milk**　　**was made to drink**

Jon san wa, | asa gohan | o | tsukuraseraremashita. |

breakfast　　**was forced to make**

/ **John was forced to make breakfast.**

§7.15 THE GIVING AND RECEIVING VERBS

Japanese has several verbs for conveying the meaning of *giving* and *receiving*. Choosing which one to use involves the relative status of the giver and receiver. It also involves the direction of the action, in the sense of giving *to* and receiving *from*.

- The following verbs are used to describe someone's giving something to you, the speaker, or to someone in your in-group, as in the diagram below the box.

To say **to give kindly (to me** or **my in-group: family, friends, etc.)**, use:
kureru
kudasaru (use for referring to superiors)

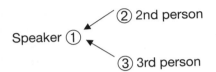

Speaker ① ← ② 2nd person
Speaker ① ← ③ 3rd person

Examples

Haha ga watakushi ni kuremashita. / **My mother gave it to me.**

my mother   me   to   gave

Kore wa tomodachi ga kureta hon desu. / **This is the book my friend gave me.**

this   friend   gave book is   me.

Sensei ga   jisho o kudasarimashita. / **The teacher gave me a dictionary.**

teacher dictionary   gave

- The following verbs are used for **I give, he gives**, etc., as in the diagram below the box.

To say **give**, use:
ageru
sashiageru (use for speaking to or referring to superiors)

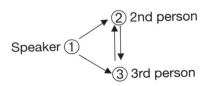

Speaker ① → ② 2nd person
Speaker ① → ③ 3rd person

Examples

Chichi ni ocha o agemashita. / **I gave my father some tea.**

father **tea** **gave**

Merī san wa, Jon san ni chizu o agemashita. / **Mary gave John a map.**

map **gave**

Tanaka san wa, shachō ni hana o sashiagemashita.

company flowers **gave**
president

/ **Mrs. Tanaka gave flowers to the company president.**

• The following verbs are used for **receive**, as in the diagram below the box.

> To say **receive**, use:
> *morau*
> *itadaku* (use for speaking to or referring to superiors)

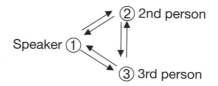

Examples

Jon san wa, tomodachi ni shīdī o moraimashita.

friend **from CD** **received**

/ **John received a CD from his friend.**

Chichi wa,   kaisha   kara bōnasu o   moraimashita.

father   company from   bonus   received

/ **Father received a bonus from the company.**

Sensei   kara   tegami o itadakimashita. / **I got a letter from the teacher.**

teacher from   letter   got

The giving and receiving verbs are often used as auxiliaries after the gerund, or -*te* form of another verb. In this usage, the relationship between the giver and the receiver is as described in the verbs given above. When speaking to or about a superior, be sure to use the appropriate verb.

- Keep in mind that these forms can mean not just giving or receiving something tangible, but also giving or receiving the action or sense of the verb.

tsukuru / **make**	*tsukutte kureru, tsukutte kudasaru*

Examples

Haha ga, watakushi ni | ban gohan | o

mother   dinner

  | tsukutte kuremashita. | / **Mother made dinner for me.**

  (kindly) made

Merī san no okāsan ga, watakushi ni sētā o

Mary   's mother   me   sweater

  | ande kudasaimashita. | / **Mary's mother knitted me a sweater.**

  (kindly) knitted

---

kau / **buy**   *katte ageru, katte sashiageru*

Examples

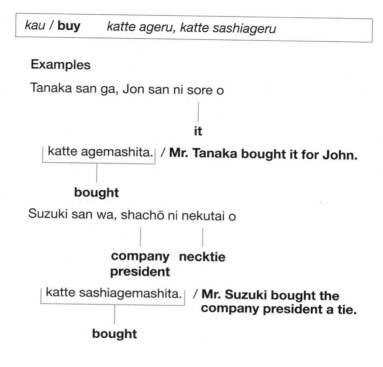

Tanaka san ga, Jon san ni sore o

it

| katte agemashita. | / **Mr. Tanaka bought it for John.**

bought

Suzuki san wa, shachō ni nekutai o

company   necktie
president

| katte sashiagemashita. | / **Mr. Suzuki bought the**
company president a tie.

bought

---

iku / **go**   *itte morau, itte itadaku*

Examples

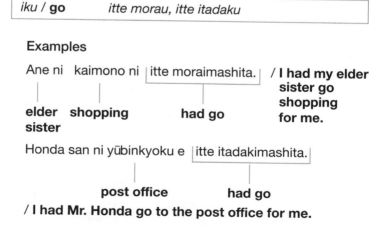

Ane ni   kaimono ni | itte moraimashita. | / **I had my elder**
sister go
shopping
elder   shopping   had go   for me.
sister

Honda san ni yūbinkyoku e | itte itadakimashita. |

post office   had go

/ **I had Mr. Honda go to the post office for me.**

§7.16 THE HONORIFIC AND HUMBLE FORMS

Using the correct language to reflect relationships is important to the Japanese. This means expressing the appropriate degree of respect or deference to the listener, and the appropriate degree of humility about oneself or one's family. The speaker's attitude toward the listener or the person being spoken about is the key. Honorific language elevates someone else; humble language lowers oneself.

Using the honorific and humble verb forms confidently takes a good deal of experience with Japanese culture, but the forms themselves are not difficult to learn.

The honorifics of verbs take several forms.

● One honorific form is the passive form itself (see **§7.12**).

Plain Form	Passive and Honorific Form
aruku / **walk**	arukareru
kaeru / **change**	kaerareru
suru / **do**	sareru
kuru / **come**	korareru

● Another set of honorific forms can be made as follows:

> *o* + infinitive + *desu*

> *yobu* / **call**   *oyobi desu* (honorific form)

Examples

Shachō ga | oyobi desu. | / **The company president is calling you.**

company president   **is calling**

Shachō ga oyobi deshita. / **The company president was calling you.**

> *o* + infinitive + *ni naru*

Examples

Shachō ga | oyobi ni narimashita. | / **The company president called you.**

called

Hon o | oyomi ni narimashita | ka. / **Have you read this book?**

book   read

> *o* + infinitive + *kudasai* / **Please (do it).**

Examples

Tanaka san o | oyobi kudasai. | / **Please call Mr. Tanaka.**

please call

Shōshō | omachi kudasai. | / **Please wait a moment.**

a little   please wait

• The humble forms can be constructed as follows:

> *o* + infinitive + *suru*

Examples

Watakushi ga Tanaka san o | oyobi shimasu. | / **I'll call Mr. Tanaka.**

will call

Hiru made ni | onaoshi shimasu. | / **I'll fix it by noon.**

noon   by   will fix

o + infinitive + *itasu*

Examples

Sugu | omochi itashimasu. | / **I'll bring it immediately.**

immediately will bring

Kasa o | okashi itashimashō ka. | / **Shall I lend you an umbrella?**

umbrella   shall lend

- Some verbs have special honorific and humble forms. Following are a few commonly used examples.

Verb	Honorific	Humble
iku / **go**	irassharu	mairu
kuru / **come**	irassharu	mairu
iru / **be**	irassharu	oru
suru / **do**	nasaru	itasu
iu / **say**	ossharu	mōsu
taberu / **eat**	meshiagaru	itadaku
miru / **see**	goran ni naru	haiken suru

§7.17 CLAUSES

Dependent Clauses

Unlike English, independent clauses in Japanese cannot be strung together in one sentence and joined by a conjunction like "and." In Japanese, the main or independent clause comes at the *end* of the sentence, and other clauses are *dependent*. Following are some basic ways in which dependent clauses are linked to the main, or independent clause.

. . . *-te/de*

- The *-te* or gerund form of the verb can be used to indicate sequential, parallel, or causal relationships of dependent clauses. Verbal adjectives (the *-kute* form) and adjectival nouns (with the *de* form of the copula) can also be used this way (See **§8**), as can nouns (with the *de* form of the copula). Look at the examples.

Sequential: As the name implies, this form is used for actions that occur in a time sequence: **first**, **then**, **then**, etc.

Example

Ginza e itte   kaimono   o shite,   uchi e   kaerimashita.

     went shopping   **did**   **home**   **returned**

/ **I went to Ginza, did some shopping, and returned home.**

Parallel: The action or meaning here is parallel, or can take place at the same time.

Examples

Yamada san wa Ginza e itte, watakushi wa Shinjuku e

               went

ikimashita. / **Mrs. Yamada went to Ginza, and I went to Shinjuku.**

went

Kono   heya wa,   hirokute   akarukute   rippa   desu.

this   room   **is spacious   is bright   gorgeous   is**

/ **This room is spacious and bright and gorgeous.**

| Causal: | The dependent clause shows the cause, the main clause shows the effect. The cause-effect relationship need not be a strong one, however, for the -*te* form to be used. |

Examples

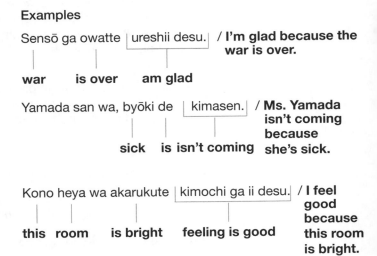

Senso ga owatte | ureshii desu.| / **I'm glad because the war is over.**

war   is over   am glad

Yamada san wa, byōki de | kimasen.| / **Ms. Yamada isn't coming because she's sick.**

sick   is isn't coming

Kono heya wa akarukute | kimochi ga ii desu.| / **I feel good because this room is bright.**

this room   is bright   feeling is good

| . . . -*tari* . . . -*tari* |

- This form is used for **do things like . . .** or **sometimes this, sometimes that**.

Examples

Shūmatsu wa, nani o shimasu ka. / **What do you do on weekends?**

weekends   what   do

Eiga o mitari, tenisu o shitari shimasu. / **I do things like seeing a movie and/or playing tennis.**

movie like tennis   like   do   tennis.
     seeing   playing

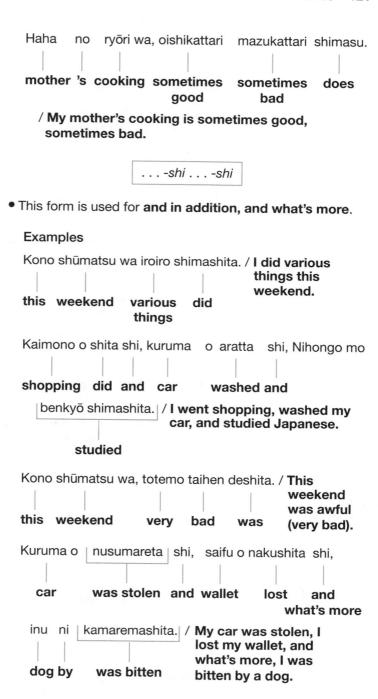

Haha no ryōri wa, oishikattari mazukattari shimasu.

mother 's cooking sometimes good — sometimes bad — does

/ My mother's cooking is sometimes good, sometimes bad.

> . . . -shi . . . -shi

- This form is used for **and in addition, and what's more.**

Examples

Kono shūmatsu wa iroiro shimashita. **/ I did various things this weekend.**

this weekend various things did

Kaimono o shita shi, kuruma o aratta shi, Nihongo mo

shopping did and car washed and

benkyō shimashita. **/ I went shopping, washed my car, and studied Japanese.**

studied

Kono shūmatsu wa, totemo taihen deshita. **/ This weekend was awful (very bad).**

this weekend very bad was

Kuruma o nusumareta shi, saifu o nakushita shi,

car was stolen and wallet lost and what's more

inu ni kamaremashita. **/ My car was stolen, I lost my wallet, and what's more, I was bitten by a dog.**

dog by was bitten

Relative Clauses

Japanese does not have relative pronouns like the English **who**, **that**, **which**, for use in relative clauses such as **The man who arrived is my friend**. Instead, the relative clause, ending with the plain form of the verb, comes *before* the word it modifies.

Examples

Watakushi ga/no itsumo   iku   restoran wa, Ginza

    I   **always   go   restaurant**

ni arimasu. / **The restaurant that I always go to is in Ginza.**

in   is

Kondo no ryokō de itta   tokoro wa, Amerika to

this   trip   went   places
time

Kanada   deshita. / **The places that I went to on this trip were America and Canada.**

Canada   were

§7.18 COMMON EXPRESSIONS WITH VERBS AND ADJECTIVES

The following forms are useful, some with verbs, some with both verbs and adjectives. If you use the *-de*, *demo*, or *dewa* forms, they can be used with nouns or adjectival nouns as well.

-temo ii desu / **It's okay if . . . You may . . .**

Examples

Takakutemo │ ii desu. │ / **It's okay (even) if it's expensive.**

if expensive is okay

Tabetemo | ii desu. | / **You may eat.**

if eat   is okay

-nakutemo ii desu / **It's okay even if it's not . . .**
You don't have to . . .

Examples

Yasukunakutemo | ii desu. | / **It's okay even if it's**
not cheap.

even if not cheap   is okay

Tabenakutemo | ii desu. | / **You don't have to eat.**

if don't eat   is okay

-tewa ikemasen / **must not**

Examples

Purezento wa okane | dewa ikemasen. | / **The gift must**
not (shouldn't)
be money.

gift   money   must not be

Tabetewa ikemasen. | / **You must not eat.**

must not eat

-nakutewa ikemasen, -nakereba narimasen / **must**

Examples

Tabenakutewa ikemasen. | / **You must eat.**

must eat

Tabenakereba narimasen. / **You must eat.**

must eat

beki desu / **should** (obligation), **ought to**

Examples

Motto | benkyō suru | | beki desu. | / **You should study more.**

more   study   should

Motto   ganbaru | beki desu. | / **You should try harder.**

more   try hard   should

hazu desu / **is expected** (no moral obligation), supposition

Examples

Mada | nete iru | |hazu desu. | / **He should still be sleeping.**

still   is sleeping   should

Kotoshi no   natsu   Nihon e iku

this year 's   summer   go

| hazu deshita. | / **I was supposed to go to Japan this summer.**

was supposed to

hō ga ii desu / **It's better (that) . . .**

Examples

Motto | benkyō shita | | hō ga ii desu. | / **You had better study harder.**

more **study** **had better**

Yasui | hō ga ii desu. | / **The cheap one is better.**

cheap **is better**

kamo shiremasen / **might, probably**

Examples

Ashita iku | kamo shiremasen. | / **I might go tomorrow.**

tomorrow **go** **might**

Mō tabeta | kamo shiremasen. | / **He might have eaten already.**

already **ate** **might**

hoshii desu / **want, need**

Examples

Okane ga | hoshii desu. | / **I need money.**

money **need**

Kōhī ga | hoshikatta desu. | / **I wanted coffee.**

coffee **wanted**

*-tai desu / **want***

Examples

Sushi ga |tabetai desu.| / **I want to eat sushi.**

want to eat

Sakana wa |tabetaku arimasen.| / **I don't want to eat fish.**

fish   **don't want to eat**

§7.19 NOMINAL-IZATION

Verbs or clauses can be nominalized, or made into nouns, by using *no* or *koto* immediately after. Note that *koto* is mor formal and can be used in the predicate; *no* is less formal and cannot be used in the predicate (see **§3.3–2**).

Examples

Watakushi wa |taberu no| ga daisuki desu. / **I like eating very much.**

eating

|Ryokō suru no| wa tanoshii desu. / **I enjoy traveling.**

traveling

|Anata ga itta koto| wa |tadashii desu.| / **What you said was right.**

What you said   **was right**

|Miru koto| wa |shinjiru koto| desu. / **Seeing is believing.**

Seeing   **believing**

|Suru yori iu no| wa kantan desu. / **It's easier said than done.**

Saying than doing

Yamada san wa | oshieru no | o yamemashita. / **Mr.**
Yamada
quit
teaching — quit — **teaching.**

§7.20
VERB CHARTS

In the following charts you will find conjugated forms of a sample of Japanese verbs.

hanasu / **to speak**

Stem: hanas-   **Transitive**

		Affirmative	Negative
Present:	Plain	hanasu	hanasanai
	Polite	hanashimasu	hanashimasen
Past:	Plain	hanashita	hanasanakatta
	Polite	hanashimashita	hanashimasen deshita
Gerund (-*te* form):		hanashite	hanasanaide hanasanakute
Presumptive:	Plain	hanasu darō	hanasanai darō
	Polite	hanasu deshō	hanasanai deshō
	Plain	hanasō	hanasumai
	Polite	hanashimashō	
Imperative:	Plain	hanase	hanasuna
	Polite	hanashite kudasai	hanasanaide kudasai
Conditional:		hanaseba hanashitara	hanasanakereba hanasanakattara

Plain Affirmative

Potential:	hanaseru	Honorific:	ohanashi ni naru
Passive:	hanasareru		ohanashi nasaru
Causative:	hanasaseru	Humble:	ohanashi suru
			ohanashi itasu
Causative Passive:	hanasaserareru		

iku / **to go**

Stem: ik-   **Intransitive**

		Affirmative	Negative
Present:	Plain	iku	ikanai
	Polite	ikimasu	ikimasen
Past:	Plain	itta	ikanakatta
	Polite	ikimashita	ikimasen deshita
Gerund (-*te* form):		itte	ikanaide ikanakute
Presumptive:	Plain	iku darō	ikanai darō
	Polite	iku deshō	ikanai deshō
	Plain	ikō	ikumai
	Polite	ikimashō	
Imperative:	Plain	ike	ikuna
	Polite	itte kudasai	ikanaide kudasai
Conditional:		ikeba ittara	ikanakereba ikanakattara

Plain Affirmative

Potential:	ikeru	Honorific:	irassharu
Passive:	ikareru		
Causative:	ikaseru	Humble:	mairu
Causative Passive:	ikaserareru		

kaeru / **to return**

Stem: kaer-   **Intransitive**

		Affirmative	Negative
Present:	Plain	kaeru	kaeranai
	Polite	kaerimasu	kaerimasen
Past:	Plain	kaetta	kaeranakatta
	Polite	kaerimashita	kaerimasen deshita
Gerund (-*te* form):		kaette	kaeranaide kaeranakute
Presumptive:	Plain	kaeru darō	kaeranai darō
	Polite	kaeru deshō	kaeranai deshō
	Plain	kaerō	kaerumai
	Polite	kaerimashō	
Imperative:	Plain	kaere	kaeruna
	Polite	kaette kudasai	kaeranaide kudasai
Conditional:		kaereba kaettara	kaeranakereba kaeranakattara

Plain Affirmative

Potential:	kaereru	Honorific:	okaeri ni naru
Passive:	kaerareru		okaeri nasaru
Causative:	kaeraseru	Humble:	———————
Causative Passive:	kaeraserareru		

kau / **to buy**

Stem: ka-   **Transitive**

		Affirmative	Negative
Present:	Plain	kau	kawanai
	Polite	kaimasu	kaimasen
Past:	Plain	katta	kawanakatta
	Polite	kaimashita	kaimasen deshita
Gerund (-*te* form):		katte	kawanaide kawanakute
Presumptive:	Plain	kau darō	kawanai darō
	Polite	kau deshō	kawanai deshō
	Plain	kaō	kaumai
	Polite	kaimashō	
Imperative:	Plain	kae	kauna
	Polite	katte kudasai	kawanaide kudasai
Conditional:		kaeba	kawanakereba
		kattara	kawanakattara

Plain Affirmative

Potential:	kaeru	Honorific:	okai ni naru
Passive:	kawareru		okai nasaru
Causative:	kawaseru	Humble:	okai suru
Causative Passive:	kawaserareru		okai itasu

kiku / **to listen, to ask, to hear**

Stem: kik-   **Transitive**

		Affirmative	Negative
Present:	Plain	kiku	kikanai
	Polite	kikimasu	kikimasen
Past:	Plain	kiita	kikanakatta
	Polite	kikimashita	kikimasen deshita
Gerund (-*te* form):		kiite	kikanaide kikanakute
Presumptive:	Plain	kiku darō	kikanai darō
	Polite	kiku deshō	kikanai deshō
	Plain	kikō	kikumai
	Polite	kikimashō	
Imperative:	Plain	kike	kikuna
	Polite	kiite kudasai	kikanaide kudasai
Conditional:		kikeba kiitara	kikanakereba kikanakattara

Plain Affirmative

Potential:	kikeru	Honorific:	okiki ni naru
Passive:	kikareru		okiki nasaru
Causative:	kikaseru	Humble:	ukagau (to ask)
Causative Passive:	kikaserareru		okiki suru (to ask)

kuru / **to come**

Stem: ku-   **Intransitive**

		Affirmative	Negative
Present:	Plain	kuru	konai
	Polite	kimasu	kimasen
Past:	Plain	kita	konakatta
	Polite	kimashita	kimasen deshita
Gerund (-*te* form):		kite	konaide konakute
Presumptive:	Plain	kuru darō	konai darō
	Polite	kuru deshō	konai deshō
	Plain	koyō	kurumai
	Polite	kimashō	
Imperative:	Plain	koi	kuruna
	Polite	kite kudasai	konaide kudasai
Conditional:		kureba	konakereba
		kitara	konakattara

Plain Affirmative

Potential:	korareru	Honorific:	irassharu
Passive:	korareru		oide ni naru
Causative:	kosaseru	Humble:	mairu
Causative Passive:	kosaserareru		

miru / **to look at, to see**

Stem: mi-   **Transitive**

		Affirmative	Negative
Present:	Plain	miru	minai
	Polite	mimasu	mimasen
Past:	Plain	mita	minakatta
	Polite	mimashita	mimasen deshita
Gerund (-*te* form):		mite	minaide
			minakute
Presumptive:	Plain	miru darō	minai darō
	Polite	miru deshō	minai deshō
	Plain	miyō	mimai
	Polite	mimashō	
Imperative:	Plain	miro	miruna
	Polite	mite kudasai	minaide kudasai
Conditional:		mireba	minakereba
		mitara	minakattara

Plain Affirmative

Potential:	mirareru	Honorific:	goran ni naru
Passive:	mirareru		goran nasaru
Causative:	misaseru	Humble:	haiken suru
Causative Passive:	misaserareru		haiken itasu

nomu / **to drink**

Stem: nom-			**Transitive**
		Affirmative	Negative
Present:	Plain	nomu	nomanai
	Polite	nomimasu	nomimasen
Past:	Plain	nonda	nomanakatta
	Polite	nomimashita	nomimasen deshita
Gerund (-*te* form):		nonde	nomanaide nomanakute
Presumptive:	Plain	nomu darō	nomanai darō
	Polite	nomu deshō	nomanai deshō
	Plain	nomō	nomumai
	Polite	nomimashō	
Imperative:	Plain	nome	nomuna
	Polite	nonde kudasai	nomanaide kudasai
Conditional:		nomeba	nomanakereba
		nondara	nomanakattara

Plain Affirmative

Potential:	nomeru	Honorific:	onomi ni naru
Passive:	nomareru		onomi nasaru
Causative:	nomaseru	Humble:	itadaku
Causative Passive:	nomaserareru		

suru / **to do, to make**

Stem: su-   **Transitive**

		Affirmative	Negative
Present:	Plain	suru	shinai
	Polite	shimasu	shimasen
Past:	Plain	shita	shinakatta
	Polite	shimashita	shimasen deshita
Gerund (-*te* form):		shite	shinaide shinakute
Presumptive:	Plain	suru darō	shinai darō
	Polite	suru deshō	shinai deshō
	Plain	shiyō	surumai
	Polite	shimashō	
Imperative:	Plain	shiro	suruna
	Polite	shite kudasai	shinaide kudasai
Conditional:		sureba	shinakereba
		shitara	shinakattara

Plain Affirmative

Potential:	dekiru	Honorific:	nasaru
Passive:	sareru		
Causative:	saseru	Humble:	itasu
Causative Passive:	saserareru		

taberu / **to eat**

Stem: tabe-   **Transitive**

		Affirmative	Negative
Present:	Plain	taberu	tabenai
	Polite	tabemasu	tabemasen
Past:	Plain	tabeta	tabenakatta
	Polite	tabemashita	tabemasen deshita
Gerund (-*te* form):		tabete	tabenaide tabenakute
Presumptive:	Plain	taberu darō	tabenai darō
	Polite	taberu deshō	tabenai deshō
	Plain	tabeyō	tabemai
	Polite	tabemashō	
Imperative:	Plain	tabero	taberuna
	Polite	tabete kudasai	tabenaide kudasai
Conditional:		tabereba	tabenakereba
		tabetara	tabenakattara

Plain Affirmative

Potential:	taberareru	Honorific:	meshiagaru
Passive:	taberareru		otabe ni naru
Causative:	tabesaseru		otabe nasaru
Causative Passive:	tabesaserareru	Humble:	itadaku

wakaru / **to understand**

Stem: wakar-   **Intransitive**

		Affirmative	Negative
Present:	Plain	wakaru	wakaranai
	Polite	wakarimasu	wakarimasen
Past:	Plain	wakatta	wakaranakatta
	Polite	wakarimashita	wakarimasen deshita
Gerund (-*te* form):		wakatte	wakaranaide wakaranakute
Presumptive:	Plain	wakaru darō	wakaranai darō
	Polite	wakaru deshō	wakaranai deshō
	Plain	wakarō	wakarumai
	Polite	wakarimashō	
Imperative:	Plain	wakare	
	Polite	wakatte kudasai	
Conditional:		wakareba	wakaranakereba
		wakattara	wakaranakattara

Plain Affirmative

Potential:	——————	Honorific:	owakari ni naru
Passive:	——————		owakari nasaru
Causative:	wakaraseru	Humble:	——————
Causative Passive:	wakaraserareru		

§8.

Adjectives

English speakers define *adjectives* as "words which modify or describe nouns."

The Japanese adjective, however, does not fit neatly into the definition of the English adjective. Therefore, speakers of English must be prepared for new ways of looking at adjectives, which in Japanese are quite unlike their English counterparts.

What are the major differences? To put it simply, Japanese adjectives fall into two groups: one group has verb-like characteristics, and the other group has noun-like characteristics. Both groups may function like English adjectives, that is, to modify nouns that follow. With this concept in mind, Japanese adjectives can be understood easily.

One group may be called *verbal adjectives*, the other *adjectival nouns*. We shall look at each group separately. First, the verbal adjectives.

Adjectives in this group, in their dictionary form, end only in *-ai, -ii, -oi,* or *-ui.* Thus, they are often referred to as *-i* adjectives.

Here are some common *-i* adjectives.

-i Adjectives	
chiisai / **small**	takai / **expensive**
yasui / **inexpensive, cheap**	ōkii / **big**
oishii / **delicious**	ii / **good, nice**
yasashii / **easy**	warui / **bad**
atarashii / **new**	muzukashii / **difficult**
omoshiroi / **interesting**	amai / **sweet**
suzushii / **cool**	wakai / **young**
hayai / **fast, early**	itai / **painful**
kuroi / **black**	shiroi / **white**

138

**§8.2–1
Noun
Modifiers**

The *-i* adjective in the forms listed above can modify a noun that follows, just as an English adjective does:

Examples

chiisai kuruma / **small car**

kuroi kutsu / **black shoes**

omoshiroi hon / **interesting book**

ii hito / **good person**

Atarashii kuruma o | kaimasu. | / **I will buy a new car.**

　　　new　　car　　will buy

Oishii kudamono o tabemashita. / **We ate some delicious fruit.**

　　　fruit

**§8.2–2
Verbal Forms**

The forms given in **§8.2** are the dictionary form of the verbal adjectives. As verbal forms, they have the characteristics of verbs, as you will see below.

> They have stems.

To form the stem, drop the final *-i*. This is the form used to make all the other forms of the adjective.

-i Adjective	Stem
akai / **red**	aka-
omoshiroi / **interesting**	omoshiro-
nagai / **long**	naga-
yasui / **cheap**	yasu-

> As is, they form the predicate.

Since the dictionary form is the plain present form of the verb, you can think of the verbal adjective as already containing in itself the grammatical form of the copula, or **is**. And, since a Japanese sentence requires a predicate but not a subject if the context is clear, each verbal adjective can constitute a sentence. There can, of course, be other elements in the sentence.

Note that these are plain forms.

Examples

Suzushii. / **It's cool.**

Muzukashii. / **It's difficult.**

Atama ga itai. / **My head hurts.**

Kono hon wa, omoshiroi. / **This book is interesting.**

> They conjugate, or change form, for different tenses and moods.

• To form the plain past tense, add *-katta* to the stem.

Plain	
Present	**Past**
suzushii / **is cool**	suzushikatta / **was cool**
oishii / **is delicious**	oishikatta / **was delicious**
chiisai / **is small**	chiisakatta / **was small**
wakai / **is young**	wakakatta / **was young**
osoi / **is slow**	osokatta / **was slow**

• To form the negative of the plain present and past, add *-ku* to the stem. Then, as with regular plain past verbs, add the appropriate form of *nai*.

Plain Negative	
Present	**Past**
suzushiku nai / **isn't cool**	suzushikunakatta / **wasn't cool**
chiisaku nai / **isn't small**	chiisakunakatta / **wasn't small**

• For the polite forms, add *desu* to the plain form for the present and the past.

Polite	
Present	**Past**
suzushii desu / **is cool**	suzushikatta desu / **was cool**
chiisai desu / **is small**	chiisakatta desu / **was small**

- To form the polite negative, use the *-ku* form, and add *arimasen* to the present, and *arimasen deshita* to the past.

Polite Negative	
Present	**Past**
suzushiku arimasen / **isn't cool**	suzushiku arimasen deshita / **wasn't cool**
chiisaku arimasen / **isn't small**	chiisaku arimasen deshita / **wasn't small**

- A variation of the polite negative forms may be formed by adding *desu* to the plain negative forms:

suzushiiku nai desu / **isn't cool**	suzushikunakatta desu / **wasn't cool**
chiisaku nai desu / **isn't small**	chiisakunakatta desu / **wasn't small**

- To form the gerund, add *-kute* to the stem.

Example

Kono hon wa omoshirokute tanoshii desu. / **This book is interesting and enjoyable.**

book   is interesting   is enjoyable

- For other verb moods, the verbal adjective forms can be expanded as follows:

Presumptive: atsui deshō / **will probably be hot**

Conditional: atsukereba / **if it were hot**

atsukunakereba / **if it were not hot**

atsukutemo / **even if it's hot**

and so forth (see **§7**).

The following examples illustrate some uses of the verbal adjective forms presented in this section.

Examples

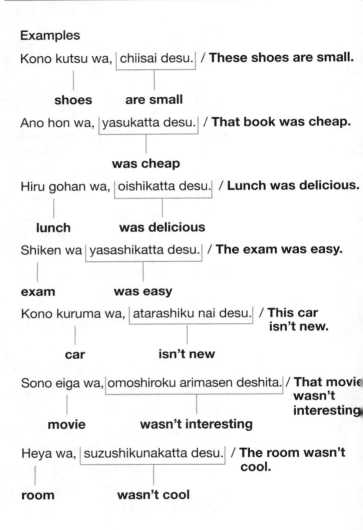

Kono kutsu wa, | chiisai desu. | / **These shoes are small.**

shoes   **are small**

Ano hon wa, | yasukatta desu. | / **That book was cheap.**

was cheap

Hiru gohan wa, | oishikatta desu. | / **Lunch was delicious.**

lunch   **was delicious**

Shiken wa | yasashikatta desu. | / **The exam was easy.**

exam   **was easy**

Kono kuruma wa, | atarashiku nai desu. | / **This car isn't new.**

car   **isn't new**

Sono eiga wa, | omoshiroku arimasen deshita. | / **That movie wasn't interesting**

movie   **wasn't interesting**

Heya wa, | suzushikunakatta desu. | / **The room wasn't cool.**

room   **wasn't cool**

**§8.2–3
Adverbial
Forms**

To form adverbs from the *-i* adjectives, just add *-ku* to the stem. Or, to put it another way, change the final *-i* to *-ku*.

Adjective	Adverb
omoshiroi / **interesting**	omoshiroku / **interesting**
hayai / **quick**	hayaku / **quick, quickly**
warui / **bad**	waruku / **bad, badly**
ii / **good**	yoku* / **well**
takai / **expensive**	takaku / **expensive**
kuroi / **black**	kuroku / **black**

*This is an irregular form.

Note how the adverbs are used in sentences. Look at the kinds of verbs typically used with adverbs, especially *naru*, **become**.

Examples

Shōsetsu ga, omoshiroku narimashita. / **The novel became interesting.**

novel   interesting   became

or

I have become interested in novels.

Hayaku ikinasai. / **Go quickly.**

quickly   go

Hayaku arukimashita. / **I walked quickly.**

Tenki ga waruku narimashita. / **The weather became bad.**

weather   bad   became

Tarō san wa, yoku | benkyō shimashita. | / **Taro studied well.**

well   studied

Yachin ga takaku   narimashita. / **The rent became expensive.**

rent   expensive   became

Doa o kuroku nurimashita. / **I painted the door black.**

door   black   painted

Ano hito wa, eigo ga yoku   wakarimasu. / **He understands English well.**

English   well understands

Yoku nemashita. / **I slept well.**

well   slept

§8.3 ADJECTIVAL NOUNS

Words in this group have noun-like characteristics and can convey adjectival meanings. When they modify nouns, they are followed by the suffix -*na*. Thus, they are often referred to as -*na* adjectives.

Here are some common -*na* adjectives.

-na **Adjectives**	
shizuka / **quiet**	kirei / **pretty**
genki / **well, healthy**	benri / **convenient**
shinsetsu / **kind**	yūmei / **famous**
jōzu / **good at**	heta / **not good at**
dame / **no good**	suki / **like**
fuben / **inconvenient**	iroiro / **various**
shōjiki / **honest**	teinei / **polite**

You may notice that these words, as translated, do not fit neatly into the English notion of adjectives. The following sections should help clarify their usage.

§8.3–1 Noun Modifiers

With the addition of *-na*, the words in the preceding chart can modify a noun that follows, just as an English adjective does. Notice that for some of the words, the English translation is adjusted slightly to fit this context.

Examples

shizukana heya / **quiet room**

kireina hana / **pretty flowers**

genkina hito / **healthy person**

benrina dōgu / **convenient tool**

shinsetsuna sensei / **kind teacher**

yūmeina joyū / **famous actress**

jōzuna kashu / **talented singer**

hetana untenshu / **bad driver**

damena hito / **no good person, bad person**

sukina tabemono / **favorite food**

fubenna jikan / **inconvenient time**

iroirona kuni / **various countries**

shōjikina seijika / **honest politician**

teineina aisatsu / **polite greetings**

This noun modifier construction is similar in form to that of the noun + *no* + noun pattern used to make compound nouns (see §4.8): *eigo no sensei* / **English teacher**, etc. With the adjectival nouns, of course, *-na* is used instead of *no*. Otherwise, the pattern is the same. This is one of the noun-like characteristics of the adjectival nouns.

Now look at some examples of this usage in sentences.

Examples

Shizukana heya ga | hoshii desu. | / **I want a quiet room.**

quiet   room   want

Sushi wa, watakushi no sukina tabemono desu. / **Sushi is my favorite food.**

favorite   food

Sore wa   fubenna   jikan desu. / **That's an inconvenient time.**

inconvenient time

Iroirona   kuni   ni ikimashita. / **I have visited various countries.**

various countries   visited

§8.3–2 Predicate Forms

The adjectival nouns form a predicate as nouns do, by adding the appropriate form of the copula, *desu* / **is, equals** (see §7.6).

Here are the basic forms of *desu*:

desu / **is, equals**		**Affirmative**	**Negative**
Present	Plain	da	dewa nai
	Polite	desu	dewa arimasen
Past	Plain	datta	dewa nakatta
	Polite	deshita	dewa arimasen deshita
Presumptive (Probable)	Plain	darō	dewa nai darō
	Polite	deshō	dewa nai deshō

The following examples illustrate how the adjectival nouns plus a form of *desu* constitute the predicate.

Examples

Kono heya wa, shizuka desu. / **This room is quiet.**

      room   **quiet**

Kōen wa, kirei dewa arimasen deshita. / **The park wasn't pretty.**

park **pretty**   **wasn't**

Chichi wa, genki desu. / **My father is healthy.**

father **healthy**

Ano hito wa, supōtsu ga heta desu. / **She isn't good at sports.**

    sports **isn't good at**

Ano yakyū no senshu wa, yūmei desu. / **That baseball player is famous.**

  baseball player **famous**

Sakana wa, suki dewa arimasen. / **I don't like fish. (Fish isn't likable.)**

fish   **don't like**

Jon san wa, Nihon ga suki desu. / **John likes Japan. (To John, Japan is likable.)**

Niku wa dame desu. / **I don't eat meat. (Meat is no good.)**

meat **is no good**

§8.3–3
Adverbial
Forms

To form adverbs from the -na adjectives, use the particle ni after the adjective.

-na Adjective	Adverb
shizuka / **quiet**	shizuka ni / **quiet, quietly**
kirei / **pretty**	kirei ni / **pretty**
genki / **healthy, well**	genki ni / **healthy, well**
shinsetsu / **kind**	shinsetsu ni / **kindly**
teinei / **polite**	teinei ni / **politely**
jōzu / **good at**	jōzu ni / **good at, well**

Look at the adverbial forms in sentences. They are often used with the verbs naru / **become** and suru / **do**.

Examples

Kanojo wa, shizuka ni arukimasu. / **She walks quietly.**
　　　　　　quietly　walks

Ano hito wa, teinei ni hanashimashita. / **He spoke politely.**
　　　　　　politely　spoke

Kanja wa, genki ni narimashita. / **The patient became healthy.**
　　　　　healthy　became

Satō san wa, eigo ga jōzu ni narimashita. / **Ms. Sato became good at English.**
　　　　　　　　　　good at

Satō san wa, eigo o jōzu ni hanashimasu. / **Mr. Sato speaks English well.**
　　　　　　　　well　speaks

Shizuka ni shinasai. / **Please be quiet.**

quiet   do

§8.4
COMPARISONS

To compare things in Japanese, the adjectives themselves do not change. Instead, there is a special pattern to learn. This pattern works for both -*i* adjectives and -*na* adjectives.

To say **A is bigger than B**, the pattern is as follows:

A *wa* B   *yori*   ōkii   desu.

than   big   is

To say **A is cheaper than B**, the pattern is the same:

A *wa* B   *yori*   yasui   desu.

than   cheap   is

Examples

Budō wa, meron   yori   yasui   desu. / **Grapes are cheaper than melons.**

grapes   melons   than   cheap   are

Tōkyō wa, Kyōto   yori   ōkii   desu. / **Tokyo is bigger than Kyoto.**

than   big   is

Kyōto wa, Tōkyō   yori   chiisai   desu. / **Kyoto is smaller than Tokyo.**

than   small   is

To understand clearly which is which in the comparison, the key is the word *yori* / **than.** Focus on this word and the English meaning, and you can quickly sort it out. If you want to say **Oranges are cheaper than apples**, start with **than apples** in English. In Japanese it becomes *ringo yori* / **apples than**, and you can see that **apples** takes the **B** slot in the pattern. The full sentence is as follows:

Another phrase is often used with this pattern, although the meaning remains the same. The words are *no hō*, plus the particle *ga.* The *no* is like the possessive particle used to link the nouns with whatever follows, and *hō* can be translated as **side** or **direction**. The pattern looks like this:

Examples

Shikago to Tōkyō to, dochira ga suki desu ka.

/ **Which do you like better, Chicago or Tokyo?**

Tōkyō no hō ga suki desu. / **I like Tokyo better.**

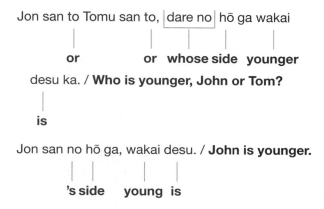

Jon san to Tomu san to, |dare no| hō ga wakai

    or   or whose side younger

desu ka. / **Who is younger, John or Tom?**

is

Jon san no hō ga, wakai desu. / **John is younger.**

    's side   young is

Notice the particle and word order changes in the following two sentences. In the first one, *no hō ga* is used, in the second, *yori* is used alone. Both sentences have the same meaning, but including *no hō ga* makes for stronger contrast in the comparison.

Examples

Basu yori, chikatetsu no hō ga benri desu. / **The subway is more convenient than the bus.**

Chikatetsu wa, basu yori benri desu. / **The subway is more convenient than the bus.**

subway   bus than

Another way to answer questions about comparisons is with a simple statement.

Examples

Ringo   to   momo   to, dochira ga suki desu ka.

apples or peaches   or   which   like

/ **Which do you like better, apples or peaches?**

Ringo ga suki desu. / **I like apples better.**

Another option is to use the word *motto*, which means **more**, for emphasis. It connotes **much** (**more**, **better**, etc.). If you use this with *no hō ga*, the emphasis is even stronger.

Examples

Ringo ga motto suki desu. / **I like apples much more.**

Ringo no hō ga, motto suki desu. / **I like apples much more.**

To convey a superlative meaning, use the word *ichiban /* **most, -est**, etc.

Examples

Dono kudamono ga ichiban suki desu ka. / **Which fruit do you like best?**

| | | | |
which   fruit   best   like

Banana ga ichiban suki desu. / **I like bananas best.**

Nihon de wa, dono tsuki ga ichiban samui desu ka.

| |
month   cold

/ **Which month is the coldest in Japan?**

§8.5 NOMINAL-IZATION

Adjectives can be *nominalized*, or made into nouns, by a simple device for each of the two kinds.

For *-i* adjectives, add *-no* to the basic, or dictionary, form.

-i Adjective	Noun Form
ōkii / **big**	ōkiino / **big one**
atarashii / **new**	atarashiino / **new one**
hayai / **fast**	hayaino / **fast one**
shiroi / **white**	shiroino / **white one**
amai / **sweet**	amaino / **sweet one**
akai / **red**	akaino / **red one**
kiiroi / **yellow**	kiiroino / **yellow one**

As with English, this form usually occurs in a context, that is, answering a question, or referring to something mutually understood.

Examples

Ringo o kudasai. / **I want some apples.**

Akaino   to   kiiroino   to,   dochira ga ii desu ka.

red ones or yellow ones or   which

/ **Which do you want, red ones or yellow ones?**

Look at two ways of saying the same thing. Note the difference in emphasis.

Atarashii eiga o mitai desu. / **I want to see a new film.**

new   film

Eiga wa, atarashiino o mitai desu. / **(As for a film), I want to see a new one.**

film   new one

Here are some more examples of nominalized adjectives used in sentences:

Examples

Kēki wa, amaino o kudasai. / **(As for the cake), give me the sweet one.**

cake sweet one

Hoteru no heya wa, chiisaino ga hoshii desu. / **(As for a hotel room), I want a small one.**

hotel   room   small one

For -na adjectives, add -no to the -na form.

-na Adjective, -na Form	Noun Form
shizukana / **quiet**	shizukanano / **quiet one**
kireina / **pretty**	kireinano / **pretty one**
yūmeina / **famous**	yūmeinano / **famous one**
sukina / **like, favorite**	sukinano / **favorite one**
benrina / **convenient**	benrinano / **convenient one**
teineina / **polite**	teineinano / **polite one, politeness**
hetana / **not good at**	hetanano / **unskillful one**

Here are some sentences with these forms. The uses are the same as for the -i adjective sentences above.

Examples

Kisha wa, | benrinano | ni | noritai desu. |

train   convenient one   want to take

/ **(As for trains), I want to take a convenient one.**

Kireinano ga | ii desu. | / **I want pretty ones.**

pretty ones   want

Teineinano wa taisetsu desu. / **Politeness is important.**

politeness   important

§9.

Adverbs

§9.1
WHAT ARE
ADVERBS?

Adverbs are words which modify or describe verbs, adjectives, or other adverbs. They indicate *time, place, manner*, and *degree*. They answer such questions as **when, where, how**, and **to what extent**.

As in English, some words in Japanese that are adverbs in one sentence can be a different part of speech in another sentence.

Examples

Kyō Tōkyō ni ikimasu. / **Today I'm going to Tokyo.**

Today

adverb

Kyō wa nichiyōbi desu. / **Today is Sunday.**

Today

noun

§9.2
ADVERBS
OF PLACE

Some of the demonstrative pronouns (see **§5.5**) function as adverbs of place.

> koko / **here**
> soko / **there**
> asoko / **over there**

Examples

Jon san ga, koko ni kimashita. / **John came here.**

Soko ni | ikitai desu. | / **I want to go there.**

Gakkō wa, asoko ni arimasu. / **The school is over there.**

§9.3 ADVERBS OF TIME

kinō / **yesterday**	
kyō / **today**	
ashita / **tomorrow**	
mainichi / **every day**	
maiasa / **every morning**	
maiban / **every night**	
ima / **now**	
saikin / **recently**	
yagate / **soon**	
sugu / **immediately**	
mada / **yet, still**	

Examples

Mainichi   shinbun o yomimasu. / **I read a newspaper every day.**

Sugu | kite kudasai. | / **Please come immediately**

Yūbin wa, mada desu. / **The mail isn't here yet.**

    | |
  mail   **not yet**

Yagate haru ga kimasu. / **Spring will come soon.**

    | | |
  soon **spring** **come**

As in English, adjectives can be made into adverbs of manner and degree:

Adjective	Adverb
hayai / **quick**	hayaku / **quick, quickly**
warui / **bad**	waruku / **bad, badly**
shizuka / **quiet**	shizuka ni / **quiet, quietly**
shinsetsu / **kind**	shinsetsu ni / **kindly**

See **§8.2–3** and **§8.3–3** for more information on the adverbial forms of adjectives.

Some of the demonstrative pronouns are adverbs of manner (see **§5.5**).

> kō / **this way, like this**
> sō / **that way, like that**
> ā / **that way, like that**
> dō / **how**

Examples

  Kō   shimashō. / **Let's do it this way.**

   | |
this way **let's do**

  Sō | shite kudasai. | / **Please do it that way.**

   | |
that way   **please do**

Ā suru   to   yoku   dekimasu. / **If you do it that way, you can do better.**

that way   if better   can do

Ōsaka ni wa, dō kimasu ka. / **How do you get to Osaka?**

how   go

Here are some other adverbs of manner and degree

amari / **not much, not often**
bakari / **only**
chotto / **a little, for a moment**
dandan / **gradually**
futsū / **usually**
hotondo / **almost, all but, hardly**
ikaga / **how**
itsumo / **always**
kitto / **certainly, surely**
mata / **again**
minna / **all**
mō / **more, already**
motto / **more**
nakanaka / **quite, rather, completely, at all**
sukoshi / **a little, few**
tabitabi / **often**
tabun / **maybe, perhaps, probably**
taihen / **very (in the sense of extreme degree, positive or negative), greatly**
taitei / **generally, mainly, perhaps, probably**
takusan / **a lot**
tamani / **occasionally**
tokidoki / **sometimes**
totemo / **very**
yoku / **well, often, much**
yukkuri / **slowly**
zenzen / **at all (with negative verbs)**
zuibun / **rather, quite**

Examples

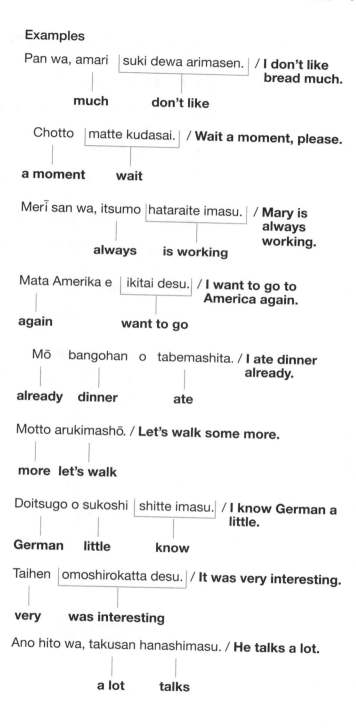

Pan wa, amari | suki dewa arimasen. | / **I don't like bread much.**

much   don't like

Chotto | matte kudasai. | / **Wait a moment, please.**

a moment   wait

Merī san wa, itsumo | hataraite imasu. | / **Mary is always working.**

always   is working

Mata Amerika e | ikitai desu. | / **I want to go to America again.**

again   want to go

Mō   bangohan o tabemashita. / **I ate dinner already.**

already dinner   ate

Motto arukimashō. / **Let's walk some more.**

more let's walk

Doitsugo o sukoshi | shitte imasu. | / **I know German a little.**

German   little   know

Taihen | omoshirokatta desu. | / **It was very interesting.**

very   was interesting

Ano hito wa, takusan hanashimasu. / **He talks a lot.**

a lot   talks

Tokidoki Tōkyō ni ikimasu. / **I sometimes go to Tokyo.**

sometimes   go

Totemo | oishikatta desu. | / **It was very delicious.**

very   was delicious

Rokugatsu wa, ame ga yoku furimasu. / **It rains often in June.**

June   rain   often falls

Yukkuri | hanashite kudasai. | / **Please speak slowly.**

slowly   speak

Eiga wa, zenzen omoshiroku | arimasen deshita. |

movie   at all   Interesting   wasn't

/ **The movie wasn't interesting at all.**

Special Topics

§10.

Numbers

Zero to One Hundred Million

**§10.1
CARDINAL
NUMBERS**

From 1 to 10 only, there are two sets of numbers. The set on the right, of Japanese origin, stops at 10. The set on the left, of Chinese origin, continues indefinitely.

rei	0	
ichi	1	hitotsu
ni	2	futatsu
san	3	mittsu
shi/yon	4	yottsu
go	5	itsutsu
roku	6	muttsu
shichi/nana	7	nanatsu
hachi	8	yattsu
ku/kyū	9	kokonotsu
jū	10	tō

To form numbers from 11 to 19, start with $\overline{ju}$, 10, and then add the number you need from the column on the left in the preceding chart.

| 11 jūichi | 12 jūni | 13 jūsan | 14 jūshi/yon | 15 jūgo |
| 16 jūroku | 17 jūshichi / nana | | 18 jūhachi | 19 jūku |

The rest is easy. Twenty is two tens, or *ni jū*, and for 21, just add the 1: *ni jū ichi*.

20 nijū	30 sanjū	40 yonjū	50 gojū
21 nijūichi	31 sanjūichi	41 yonjūichi	51 gojūichi
60 rokujū	70 nanajū	80 hachijū	90 kyūjū
61 rokujūichi	71 nanajūichi	81 hachijūichi	91 kyūjūichi

With 100, *hyaku*, and 1,000, *sen*, the pattern is basically the same, but there are some sound changes, as you will see in the chart below:

100	hyaku	1,000	sen
200	nihyaku	2,000	nisen
300	sanbyaku	3,000	sanzen
400	yonhyaku	4,000	yonsen
500	gohyaku	5,000	gosen
600	roppyaku	6,000	rokusen
700	nanahyaku	7,000	nanasen
800	happyaku	8,000	hassen
900	kyūhyaku	9,000	kyūsen

Japanese uses 10,000 as a counting unit. Each unit of 10,000 is called *man*.

So 10,000 is *ichiman*, 20,000 is *niman*, 100,000 is *jūman*, 200,000 is *nijūman*, 1,000,000 is *hyakuman* (100 units of 10,000). This continues until 100,000,000, *ichioku*.

**§10.2
ORDINAL
NUMBERS**

The ordinal numbers are formed by adding *banme* to the cardinal numbers.

first	ichibanme	**sixth**	rokubanme
second	nibanme	**seventh**	nanabanme
third	sanbanme	**eighth**	hachibanme
fourth	yonbanme	**ninth**	kyūbanme
fifth	gobanme	**tenth**	jūbanme

To continue, follow the pattern for the cardinal numbers, adding *banme*. **Eleventh** is *jūichibanme*, **twelfth** is *jūnibanme*, and so forth.

§11.

Telling Time

To express time in Japanese, we start with a list of the **hours**, then a list of the **minutes**, and then we put them together.

Here are the **hours**:

1 o'clock	ichiji	7 o'clock	shichiji
2 o'clock	niji	8 o'clock	hachiji
3 o'clock	sanji	9 o'clock	kuji
4 o'clock	yoji	10 o'clock	jūji
5 o'clock	goji	11 o'clock	jūichiji
6 o'clock	rokuji	12 o'clock	jūniji

Now the **minutes**:

1 minute	ippun	15 minutes	jūgofun
2 minutes	nifun	16 minutes	jūroppun
3 minutes	sanpun	17 minutes	jūnanafun
4 minutes	yonpun	18 minutes	jūhappun
5 minutes	gofun	19 minutes	jūkyūfun
6 minutes	roppun	20 minutes	nijūppun
7 minutes	nanafun	21 minutes	nijūippun
8 minutes	happun	22 minutes	nijūnifun
9 minutes	kyūfun	23 minutes	nijūsanpun
10 minutes	juppun	24 minutes	nijūyonpun
11 minutes	jūippun	25 minutes	nijūgofun
12 minutes	jūnifun	30 minutes	sanjuppun
13 minutes	jūsanpun	40 minutes	yonjuppun
14 minutes	jūyonpun	50 minutes	gojuppun

Now we can put them together. Say the hour first, then the minutes, then add *desu*:

Examples

Nanji desu ka. / **What time is it?**

Jūji jūgofun desu. / **It's 10:15.**

- Using *sugi*, which means **past** or **after**, is optional.

Jūji jūgofun   sugi   desu. / **It's 10:15.**

after

- At 15 minutes before the hour, start using *mae*, which means **to** or **before**.

Jūji jūgofun mae desu. / **It's a quarter to ten.**

before

- *Han* means **half**, as in **half past** the hour.

Goji desu.	It's 5 o'clock.
Goji gofun desu.	It's 5:05.
Goji juppun desu.	It's 5:10.
Goji jūgofun desu.	It's 5:15.
Goji nijuppun desu.	It's 5:20.
Goji nijūgofun desu.	It's 5:25.
Goji han desu.	It's 5:30.
Goji sanjūgofun desu.	It's 5:35.
Goji yonjuppun desu.	It's 5:40.
Goji yonjūgofun desu.	It's 5:45.
Rokuji jūgofun mae desu.	It's a quarter to six.
Rokuji juppun mae desu.	It's 5:50/ten to six.
Rokuji gofun mae desu.	It's 5:55/five to six.

- *Gozen* is A.M. *Gogo* is P.M. Say them *before* you say the hour.

Examples

Gozen kuji desu. / **It's 9 A.M.**

|
A.M.

Gogo jūji desu. / **It's 10 P.M.**

|
P.M.

For time schedules, as in railway and airline timetables, numbers 1 to 59 are used for minutes, *not* **a quarter to** or **ten to** the hour.

Transportation timetables are based on the 24-hour clock. Airline and train schedules are expressed in terms of a point within a 24-hour sequence.

Examples

Watakushi no kisha wa, jūsanji yonjūhappun ni demasu. / **My train departs at 13:48.**

Watakushi no hikōki wa, jūji gojūsanpun ni tsukimasu. / **My plane arrives at 10:53.**

§12.

Classifiers

To count things in Japanese, you use special classifiers, or counters. Here are some of the most common ones:

Counting Different Kinds of Things

People				
1 hitori	2 futari	3 sannin	4 yonin	5 gonin
6 rokunin	7 nananin	8 hachinin	9 kunin	10 jūnin

Long, thin objects (pencils, bottles, trees, etc.)				
1 ippon	2 nihon	3 sanbon	4 yonhon	5 gohon
6 roppon	7 nanahon	8 happon	9 kyūhon	10 jūppon

Bound objects (books, magazines, notebooks, etc.)				
1 issatsu	2 nisatsu	3 sansatsu	4 yonsatsu	5 gosatsu
6 rokusatsu	7 nanasatsu	8 hassatsu	9 kyūsatsu	10 jussatsu

Thin, flat objects (paper, bills, cloth, tickets, dishes, etc.)				
1 ichimai	2 nimai	3 sanmai	4 yomai	5 gomai
6 rokumai	7 nanamai	8 hachimai	9 kyūmai	10 jūmai

Liquid or dry measures (glasses or cups of water, coffee, tea, etc.)				
1 ippai	2 nihai	3 sanbai	4 yonhai	5 gohai
6 roppai	7 nanahai	8 happai	9 kyūhai	10 juppai

Houses, buildings, etc.				
1 ikken	2 niken	3 sangen	4 yonken	5 goken
6 rokken	7 nanaken	8 hakken	9 kyūken	10 jukken

Floors of buildings				
1 ikkai	2 nikai	3 sangai	4 yonkai	5 gokai
6 rokkai	7 nanakai	8 hakkai	9 kyūkai	10 jukkai

Animals, fish, insects				
1 ippiki	2 nihiki	3 sanbiki	4 yonhiki	5 gohiki
6 roppiki	7 nanahiki	8 happiki	9 kyūhiki	10 juppiki

Small objects not in categories listed above (apples, candy, etc.)		
1 ikko / hitotsu	2 niko / futatsu	3 sanko / mittsu
4 yonko / yottsu	5 goko / itsutsu	6 rokko / muttsu
7 nanako / nanatsu	8 hakko / yattsu	9 kyūko / kokonotsu
10 jukko / tō		

To form the question word for the classifiers, do the following:

• Start with the word for counting three of anything.

• Instead of *san*, use *nan*.

For example:

sangen becomes *nangen* / **how many houses, buildings, etc.**

sanbai becomes *nanbai* / **how many glasses, cups, etc.**

Examples

hito futari / **two people**

inu sanbiki / **three dogs**

hito futari to inu sanbiki / **two people and three dogs**

Tēburu no ue niwa, orenji ga mittsu to hon ga nisatsu arimasu. / **Three oranges and two books are on the table.**

Kōen niwa, hito ga nananin to inu ga gohiki imasu. / **Seven people and five dogs are in the park.**

§13.

Days, Months, Seasons, and the Weather

getsuyōbi / **Monday**   mokuyōbi / **Thursday**
kayōbi / **Tuesday**   kinyōbi / **Friday**
suiyōbi / **Wednesday**   doyōbi / **Saturday**
              nichiyōbi / **Sunday**

        asa / **morning**   gogo / **afternoon**
        yūgata / **evening**   yoru / **night**

Related Expressions

Kyō wa, nani yōbi desu ka. / **What day is today?**
Kyō wa, _____ desu. / **It's _____.**

ichinichi / **a day**
kyō / **today**
kinō / **yesterday**
ototoi / **the day before
    yesterday**
ashita / **tomorrow**
asatte / **the day after
    tomorrow**
shū / **week**
konshū / **this week**
raishū / **next week**
senshū / **last week**
isshūkan / **for one week**
nishūkan / **for two weeks**
yūgata / **in the early
    evening**
yoru / **in the evening, at
    night**

asa made ni / **by morning**
kayōbi made ni / **by
    Tuesday**
futsuka kan / **for two days**
ichi nichi de / **in one day**
futsuka de / **in two days**
isshūkan de / **in one week**
nishūkan de / **in two weeks**
mikka mae / **three days ago**
kesa / **this morning**
kyō no gogo / **this
    afternoon**
konban / **tonight, this
    evening**
ashita no ban / **tomorrow
    night**
gozen chū / **in the morning**
gogo / **in the afternoon**

hiruni / **at noon**
heijitsu / **weekday**
shūmatsu / **weekend**
yasumi / **day off**
kyūjitsu / **holiday**
shigoto bi/ **work day**
mainichi / **every day**

kyō kara isshūkan go / **a week from today**
kyō kara / **from today on**
ichinichi ni tsuki / **per day**
kyō jū ni / **during the day**
konshū jū ni / **during the week**

13.2 MONTHS OF THE YEAR

ichigatsu / **January**	shichigatsu / **July**
nigatsu / **February**	hachigatsu / **August**
sangatsu / **March**	kugatsu / **September**
shigatsu / **April**	jūgatsu / **October**
gogatsu / **May**	jūichigatsu / **November**
rokugatsu / **June**	jūnigatsu / **December**

nan gatsu / **which month**

13.3 DAYS OF THE MONTH

tsuitachi / **1st**	jūrokunichi / **16th**
futsuka / **2nd**	jūshichinichi / **17th**
mikka / **3rd**	jūhachinichi / **18th**
yokka / **4th**	jūkunichi / **19th**
itsuka / **5th**	hatsuka* / **20th**
muika / **6th**	nijūichinichi / **21st**
nanoka / **7th**	nijūninichi / **22nd**
yōka / **8th**	nijūsannichi / **23rd**
kokonoka / **9th**	nijūyokka* / **24th**
tōka / **10th**	nijūgonichi / **25th**
jūichinichi / **11th**	nijūrokunichi / **26th**
jūninichi / **12th**	nijūshichinichi / **27th**
jūsannichi / **13th**	nijūhachinichi / **28th**
jūyokka* / **14th**	nijūkunichi / **29th**
jūgonichi / **15th**	sanjūnichi / **30th**
	sanjūichinichi / **31st**

nan nichi / **which day**

(*irregular)

§13.4 COUNTING DAYS

ichinichi / **one day**	nanoka / **seven days**
futsuka / **two days**	yōka / **eight days**
mikka / **three days**	kokonoka / **nine days**
yokka / **four days**	tōka / **ten days**
itsuka / **five days**	jūichinichi / **eleven days**
muika / **six days**	jūninichi / **twelve days**

Related Expressions

nikagetsu mae / **2 months ago**
sengetsu / **last month**
kongetsu / **this month**
raigetsu / **next month**
_____ gatsu chū ni / **during the month of** _____
_____ gatsu irai / **since the month of** _____
_____ gatsu ni / **for the month of** _____
mai tsuki / **every month**
ikkagetsu ni tsuki / **per month**
ikkagetsu / **one month**
sūkagetsu / **a few months**
Kyō wa, nan nichi desu ka. / **What's today's date?**
Kyō wa, _____ desu. / **Today is** _____.
gogatsu tsuitachi, getsuyōbi / **Monday, May 1**
rokugatsu futsuka, kayōbi / **Tuesday, June 2**

Note: For these expressions, use the days of the month listed in **§13.3.**

§13.5 SEASONS

haru / **spring**	aki / **fall**
natsu / **summer**	fuyu / **winter**

Related Expressions

Haru desu. / **It's spring.**
Natsu desu. / **It's summer.**
Aki desu. / **It's fall.**
Fuyu desu. / **It's winter.**

**13.5
THE WEATHER**

Tenki wa dō desu ka. / **How's the weather?**

Samui desu. / **It's cold.**

Totemo samui desu. / **It's very cold.**

Yuki ga futte imasu. / **It's snowing.**

Atatakai desu. / **It's warm.**

Hi ga tette imasu. / **It's sunny.**

Atsui desu. / **It's hot.**

Shikke ga takai desu. / **It's humid.**

Mushiatsui desu. / **It's hot and humid.**

Ii tenki desu. / **It's a beautiful day.**

Ame ga futte imasu. / **It's raining.**

Arashi desu. / **It's stormy.**

Kaminari ga natte, inazuma ga hikatte imasu. / **It's thundering and lightning.**

Suzushii desu. / **It's cool.**

Kiri desu. / **It's foggy.**

Ame ga, hageshiku futte imasu. / **It's raining heavily.**

§14.

Family Relationships

Choose a term from the appropriate column in the chart below when talking about family members. In Japanese, the terms for family relationships differ according to whether you are talking about your own family to someone else, or about the other person's family. You refer to your own family with a set of neutral forms, to another person's family with a set of honorific terms.

Family Member	Talking About Your Family	Talking About Another's Family
grandfather	sofu	ojiisan
grandmother	sobo	obāsan
father	chichi	otōsan
mother	haha	okāsan
husband	otto/shujin	goshujin
wife	tsuma	okusan
uncle	oji	ojisan
aunt	oba	obasan
son	musuko	musukosan
daughter	musume	ojōsan
cousin	itoko	itoko
elder brother	ani	oniisan
younger brother	otōto	otōtosan
elder sister	ane	onēsan
younger sister	imōto	imōtosan
grandchild	mago	omagosan
nephew	oi	oigosan
niece	mei	meigosan

§15.

Useful Words and Phrases

You will find this section useful in communicating with the Japanese. Just find the category you want, and choose the expression you need!

To begin, you should know that Japanese does not have a word that is the equivalent of the English word **Hello**. Instead, use the words for **Good morning, Good afternoon**, etc.

> Ohayō gozaimasu. / **Good morning.**
>
> Konnichiwa. / **Good afternoon.**
>
> Konbanwa. / **Good evening.**
>
> Oyasuminasai. / **Good night.** (This is used at the end of the evening, or at bedtime.)
>
> Sayōnara. / **Goodbye.**

Japanese has no equivalent for the English expression **How are you?** that is used as a daily greeting. The following expression is used only when you have not seen someone for a while.

> Ogenki desu ka. / **How are you?**
>
> Hai, okagesama de. / **Fine, thank you.**

You will find these expressions handy in daily life.

Hai. / **Yes.**

Iie. / **No.**

san / **Mr., Mrs., Miss, Ms.**

Dōmo arigatō. / **Thank you.**

175

Iie, dō itashimashite. / **You're welcome.**

Sumimasen. / **Excuse me** (to get someone's attention).

Gomennasai. / **I'm sorry** (apology).

Onegai shimasu. / **Please** (request).

Dōzo. / **Please** (go ahead, begin).

Moshi moshi. / **Hello.** (This is used for telephone calls, or for getting someone's attention.)

Sumimasen ga. / **Pardon me, but** _____.

Daijōbu desu. / **It's all right.**

Yorokonde. / **With pleasure.**

Ii desu yo. / **I don't mind.**

Ā, sō desu ka. / **Oh, I see.**

Ikimashō ka. / **Shall we go?**

Sā. / **Let's (go/eat/etc.)**

Iie, kekkō desu. / **No, thank you.**

Sō da to omoimasu. / **I think so.**

Sō omoimasen. / **I don't think so.**

Omoshiroi desu. / **It's interesting.**

Owarimashita. / **It's over / I'm finished.**

Hai, sō desu. / **Yes, it is.**

Iie, chigaimasu. / **No, it isn't.**

Chotto, matte kudasai. / **Just a moment, please.**

Sugu, onegai shimasu. / **Right away** (request).

Soredewa nochi hodo. / **See you later.**

Soredewa mata ashita. / **See you tomorrow.**

Wakarimasu ka. / **Do you understand?**

Hai, wakarimasu. / **Yes, I understand.**

Iie, wakarimasen. / **No, I don't understand.**

Eigo ga wakarimasu ka. / **Do you understand English?**

Nihongo ga, sukoshi hanasemasu. / **I speak a little Japanese.**

Nihongo wa, wakarimasen. / **I don't understand Japanese.**

Mō ichido onegai shimasu. / **Could you repeat it, please?**

Mō sukoshi, yukkuri hanshite kudasai. / **Please speak slowly.**

Eigo o hanashimasu ka. / **Do you speak English?**

Kore wa, Nihongo de nan to iimasu ka. / **What's this called in Japanese?**

Kore wa, nan to iimasu ka. / **What do you call this?**

Sumimasen ga, tasukete itadakemasen ka. / **Excuse me, could you help me, please?**

§15.3 SOME QUESTIONS AND QUESTION WORDS

Dō ka, shimashita ka. / **What's the matter?**

Kore wa, nan desu ka. / **What's this?**

Itsu. / **When?**

Doko. / **Where?**

Naze. / Dōshite. / **Why?**

Dare. / Donata. / **Who?**

Dore. / Dochira. / **Which?**

Nani. / **What?**

Dono kurai. / **How much?**

Ikura. / **How much (money)?**

§15.4 YOUR PERSONAL CONDITION

Nodo ga, kawaite imasu. / **I'm thirsty.**

Onaka ga, suite imasu. / **I'm hungry.**

Onaka ga, ippai desu. / **I'm full.**

Tsukarete imasu. / **I'm tired.**

Nemui desu. / **I'm sleepy.**

Byōki desu. / **I'm sick.**

Genki desu. / **I'm fine.**

Daijōbu desu. / **I'm all right.**

§15.5 INTRO-DUCTIONS

Proper introductions are important in Japan. When possible, it's preferable to have a Japanese friend introduce you to another Japanese. If not, you will find the expressions you need below.

Ano kata wa, donata desu ka. / **Who is that?**

Ano kata wa, donata ka gozonji desu ka. / **Do you know who that is?**

Ano kata ni, ome ni kakaritai no desu ga. / **I would like to meet him / her.**

Ano kata ni, shōkai shite itadakemasen ka. / **Would you introduce me to him / her?**

Totsuzen shitsurei desu ga, jiko shōkai shitemo yoroshii desu ka. / **Pardon me, may I introduce myself?**

Watakushi no namae wa ___ desu. / **My name is ___**

Onamae o ukagaemasu ka. / **May I ask your name?**

Onamae wa. / **What's your name?**

Hajimemashite. Dōzo yoroshiku. / **How do you do?**

Hajimemashite. Kochira koso yoroshiku. / **How do you do?** (reply)

Ome ni kakarete, kōei desu. / **I'm honored to meet you.**

Yoroshiku onegai shimasu. / **I'm glad to meet you.**

meishi / **business card**

Meishi o dōzo. / **Here's my card.**

Arigatō gozaimasu. / **Thank you very much.**

Watakushi no mo dōzo. / **Here's mine.**

Meishi o chōdai dekimasu ka. / **May I have your card?**

Kore ga watakushi no denwa bangō desu. / **This is my telephone number.**

Kore ga watakushi no keitai no bangō desu. / **This is my cell phone number.**

Kore ga watakushi no īmēru adoresu desu. / **This is my e-mail address.**

Denwa bangō/keitai no bangō/ īmēru adoresu o chōdai dekimasu ka. / **May I have your telephone number/cell phone number/e-mail address?**

§16.

Borrowed Words

Countless words borrowed from English are in everyday use in Japan. But even for an English speaker, there are pitfalls. Why? With borrowed words in Japan, you can never assume that they have made the trip across the Pacific intact.

Trust These!

These words *are* what they seem. If you can understand the pronunciation, you have the meaning.

orenji / **orange**	bīru / **beer**
kōhī / **coffee**	pinku / **pink**
poketto / **pocket**	gasorin / **gasoline**
takushī / **taxi**	basu / **bus**
rajio / **radio**	tomato / **tomato**
banana / **banana**	batā / **butter**
kukkī / **cookie**	sūpu / **soup**
reinkōto / **raincoat**	beddo / **bed**

Careful!

Some element in each of these words connects it to the original meaning.

wāpuro / **word processor**	hankachi / **handkerchief**
pasokon / **personal computer**	gurēdo appu / **upgrade (air travel)**
waishatsu / **dress shirt**	irasuto / **illustration**
sūpā / **supermarket**	amefuto / **American football**
basuke / **basketball**	
puro / **professional**	magu kappu / **mug**
depāto / **department store**	rimokon / **remote control**

179

> Made in Japan!

With words like these, all bets are off. Don't even think of them as coming from English. How different *are* they? If you are invited for *baikingu*, don't put on your biking clothes. You are going for some smorgasbord, *not* biking!

baikingu / **smorgasbord (Viking)**
mōningu sābisu / **breakfast special**
kēki baikingu / **dessert smorgasbord**
manshon / **condominium, modern apartment**
manshon rifōmu / **condominium renovations**
merumaga / **e-mail newsletter**
entame / **entertainment**
wanpīsu / **dress (one piece)**

Here are some more borrowed words. The meaning in parentheses lets you see the origin. Enjoy them, but remember the tips you have just seen!

anime / **animation**
ankēto / **questionnaire**
baburu (keizai) / **bubble economy**
bakansu / **vacation** / (*vacances*—French)
bea / **wage hike** / (base-up)
bigguban / **financial reform** / (big bang)
defure supairaru / **deflationary spiral**
dejikame / **digital camera**
enerugisshu / **energetic**
esute / **total beauty care** / (*esthetique*—French)
furī daiyaru / **toll-free**
furītā / **free-lancer** / (free + *Arbeiter*—German)
furonto / **front desk, reception desk**
kānabi / **car navigation system**
koin randorī / **laundromat** / (coin laundry)
konbini / **convenience store**
masukomi / **mass media**

meiku / **makeup**

mōningu koru / **wake-up call**

nego / **negotiation**

nōsurību / **sleeveless**

nōto pasokon / **notebook computer**

ōdāmeido / **custom-made**

ōtobai / **motorcycle**

panku / **flat tire** / (puncture)

pansuto / **pantyhose** / (panty stockings)

pāto / **part-time job**

penki / **paint**

pokeberu / **beeper** / (pocket bell)

poruno / **pornography**

rafu / **casual (fashion)** / (rough)

reji / **cashier**

reshipi / **recipe**

rifōmu / **alteration, renovation** / (reform)

rinyūaru / **store renovation** / (renewal)

risutora / **restructuring of business** / (restructuring)

sekuhara / **sexual harassment**

shīru / **sticker**

sumāto / **stylish, slim** / (smart)

supakon / **supercomputer**

supattsu / **tights**

toranpu / **playing cards**

uirusu / **virus**

wakuchin / **vaccine**

wan puraisu shoppu / **dollar shop** / (one-price shop)

wanrūmu manshon / **studio apartment** / (one-room mansion)

zenekon / **general contractor**

§17.

Synonyms

Synonyms are words with the same or nearly the same meaning.

benkyō suru / manabu / **to study**
betsu no / chigatta / **different**
chōshoku / asagohan / **breakfast**
chūshoku / hirugohan / **lunch**
daidokoro / okatte / **kitchen**
denwa suru / denwa o kakeru / **to telephone**
depāto / hyakkaten / **department store**
furoba / yokushitsu / **bathroom**
genzai / ima / **now**
hajime / saisho / **beginning**
hashiru / kakeru / **to run**
hataraku / shigoto suru / **to work**
henna / okashina / **strange**
honya / shoten / **bookstore**
isu / koshikake / **chair**
kaeru / modoru / **to return**
kaiko sareru / kubi ni naru / **to be fired**
katazukeru / seiton suru / **to clean up**
kau / kōnyū suru / **to buy**
keikan / omawarisan / **police officer**
keredomo / dakedo / **but**
ki o tsukeru / chūi suru / **to be careful**
kireina / utsukushii / **beautiful**
komu / konzatsu suru / **to be crowded**
kūkō / hikōjō / **airport**
kuruma / jidōsha / **car**
mata / futatabi / **again**

michi / dōro / **road**

muzukashii / konnan na / **difficult**

nakusu / ushinau / **to lose**

nedan / kakaku / **price**

Nihon ryōri / washoku / **Japanese food**

otearai / toire / **toilet**

otozureru / hōmon suru / **to visit**

owari / saigo / **ending**

seiyō ryōri / yōshoku / **western food**

shikujiru / shippai suru / **to fail**

shinsetsuna / yasashii / **kind**

shuppatsu suru / deru / **to depart**

sotto / shizuka ni / **quietly**

sugu ni / tadachi ni / **immediately**

tabi / ryokō / **travel**

tada no / muryō no / **free (cost)**

tasu / kuwaeru / **to add**

tōchaku suru / tsuku / **to arrive**

tomaru / shukuhaku suru / **to stay (overnight)**

totemo / hijō ni / **very**

uchi / ie / **house**

wakaru / rikai suru / **to understand**

waribiku / makeru / **to discount**

yakkyoku / kusuriya / **pharmacy**

yamai / byōki / **illness**

yasumu / kyūkei suru / **to rest**

yūshoku / bangohan / **dinner**

§18.

Antonyms

Antonyms are words with opposite meanings.

agaru / **to rise**	sagaru / **to fall**
akarui / **bright**	kurai / **dark**
atsui / **hot (weather)**	samui / **cold (weather)**
atsui / **hot**	tsumetai / **cold**
atsui / **thick**	usui / **thin**
futoi / **thick**	hosoi / **thin**
genki / **well**	byōki / **ill**
hajimaru / **to begin**	owaru / **to end**
hashiru / **to run**	aruku / **to walk**
hayai / **early**	osoi / **late**
hayai / **fast**	osoi / **slow**
hirou / **to pick up**	suteru / **to discard**
ii / **good**	warui / **bad**
jōzu / **good at**	heta / **poor at**
katai / **hard**	yawarakai / **soft**
kiru / **to put on**	nugu / **to take off**
manabu / **to study**	asobu / **to play**
mitsukeru / **to find**	nakusu / **to lose**
nagai / **long**	mijikai / **short**
noboru / **to climb**	kudaru / **to descend**
noru / **to get on**	oriru / **to get off**
omoi / **heavy**	karui / **light**
onaji / **same**	chigau / **different**
sannsei suru / **to agree**	hanntai suru / **to oppose**
seikō suru / **to succeed**	shippai suru / **to fail**
shizuka / **quiet**	urusai / **noisy**
shuppatsu suru / **to depart**	tōchaku suru / **to arrive**
surudoi / **sharp**	nibui / **dull**

takai / **high**	hikui / **low**
takai / **expensive**	yasui / **cheap**
tsukeru / **to turn on**	kesu / **to turn off**
warau / **to laugh**	naku / **to cry**
yasashii / **easy**	muzukashii / **difficult**
yorokobu / **to be pleased**	kanashimu / **to be sad**

§19.

Short Vowel, Long Vowel

Although the words in the two columns look alike, a closer look shows those on the right contain one or more long vowel. Hold these vowel sounds twice as long as the short vowels.

goi / **vocabulary**	gōi / **agreement**
jōho / **concession**	jōhō / **information**
josei / **woman**	jōsei / **situation**
kokyō / **hometown**	kōkyō / **public**
koritsu / **isolation**	kōritsu / **publicly funded**
koru / **to get into**	kōru / **to freeze**
koshō / **breakdown**	kōshō / **negotiation**
kuki / **stem**	kūki / **air**
kyoka suru / **to permit**	kyōka suru / **to strengthen**
roka suru / **to filter**	rōka suru / **to age**
sato / **village**	satō / **sugar**
seito / **student**	seitō / **political party**
shochi suru / **to deal with**	shōchi suru / **to consent**
shoki no / **early**	shōki no / **sane**
shomei suru / **to sign**	shōmei suru / **to prove**
soshiki / **organization**	sōshiki / **funeral**
suji / **plot**	sūji / **figure**
teki / **enemy**	teiki / **regular**
toki / **time**	tōki / **registration**
toru / **to take**	tōru / **to go through**
toshi / **year**	tōshi / **investment**
tsuchi / **soil**	tsūchi / **notice**
yoji / **four o'clock**	yōji / **business**
yuki / **snow**	yūki / **courage**
yume / **dream**	yūmei / **fame**

§20.

Double Consonants

Although the words in the two columns look similar, those on the right contain a double consonant. Don't say the consonant twice: just hold the sound twice as long.

boshū suru / **to recruit**	bosshū suru / **to confiscate**
bushi / **samurai**	busshi / **goods**
dakai suru / **to break through**	dakkai suru / **to regain**
fukyū suru / **to become widespread**	fukkyū suru / **to be restored**
futō / **unfair**	futtō / **boiling**
gashō / **art dealer**	gasshō / **chorus**
haken suru / **to dispatch**	hakken suru / **to discover**
haki suru / **to cancel**	hakki suru / **to display**
jikan / **time**	jikkan / **sense of reality**
jiken / **incident**	jikken / **experiment**
jikō / **matters**	jikkō / **execution**
jitai / **situation**	jittai / **actual condition**
kaki / **summertime**	kakki / **vigor**
keshō / **makeup**	kesshō / **finals**
kokyō / **hometown**	kokkyō / **border**
koshi / **hips**	kosshi / **gist**
machi / **town**	matchi / **matches**
maki / **firewood**	makki / **the last stage**
niki / **two terms**	nikki / **diary**
oto / **sound**	otto / **one's own husband**
saka / **slope**	sakka / **writer**
sasuru / **to stroke**	sassuru / **to guess**
seken / **society**	sekken / **soap**
shiki / **four seasons**	shikki / **lacquerware**

shisaku suru / **to contemplate**

shissaku suru / **to make a mistake**

shoki / **the early stage**

shokki / **tableware**

shuchō suru / **to assert**

shutchō suru / **to go on a business trip**

§21.

Same Pronunciation, Different Meaning

These words have the same pronunciation but different meanings. Note that they are not homonyms. Although the romaji and hiragana spellings are the same, the kanji, or Japanese characters, are different.

en / **yen** / **relation**
ha / **tooth** / **leaf**
hana / **flower** / **nose**
han-ei / **reflection** / **prosperity**
hi / **fire** / **day**
kai / **shellfish** / **meeting**
kakeru / **to hang** / **to run**
kami / **paper** / **hair**
kawa / **leather** / **river**
kaze / **wind** / **cold**
ki / **spirit** / **tree**
kiji / **article** / **cloth**
kikai / **opportunity** / **machine**
kiku / **to listen to** / **to be effective**
kōgyō / **industry** / **mining**
kōtei / **school yard** / **affirmation**
kumo / **cloud** / **spider**
kyōchō suru / **to emphasize** / **to coordinate**
me / **eye** / **bud**
nami / **wave** / **ordinary**
shima / **island** / **stripe**
shita / **under** / **tongue**
tomaru / **to stay (overnight)** / **to stop**
utsu / **to hit** / **to shoot**
utsusu / **to transfer** / **to photograph**

§22.

Pitch Accent: Different Pitch, Different Meaning

English uses stress, or emphasis, to accent syllables; Japanese uses pitch, or tone. The standard dialect has two pitch levels, high and low. For the English speaker learning Japanese, this takes practice. The lists below show you one aspect of how pitch accent works. On the left, pronounce the syllables at about the same level. On the right, use a higher pitch, or tone, for the capitalized syllables. This difference in pitch results in a different meaning.

ame	(ah-meh) / **candy**	(AH-meh) / **rain**
asa	(ah-sah) / **morning**	(ah-SAH) / **linen**
fuku	(foo-koo) / **to wipe**	(FOO-koo) / **to blow**
hashi	(hah-shee) / **end**	(HAH-shee) / **chopsticks**
		(hah-SHEE) / **bridge**
ima	(ee-mah) / **now**	(ee-MAH) / **living room**
kakeru	(kah-keh-roo) / **to lack**	(kah-KEH-roo) / **to gamble**
kaki	(kah-kee) / **persimmon**	(KAH-kee) / **oyster**
kami	(kah-mee) / **paper**	(KAH-mee) / **god**
	(kah-mee) / **hair**	
kau	(kah-oo) / **to buy**	(KAH-oo) / **to keep (a pet)**
kiru	(kee-roo) / **to cut**	(kee-ROO) / **to put on**
kisha	(kee-shah) / **train**	(KEE-shah) / **reporter**
michi	(mee-chee) / **street**	(MEE-chee) / **unknown**
sake	(sah-keh) / *sake*	(SAH-keh) / **salmon**
saku	(sah-koo) / **to bloom**	(SAH-koo) / **to tear**
seki	(seh-kee) / **seat**	(seh-KEE) / **cough**
shiro	(shee-roh) / **white**	(shee-ROH) / **castle**

LET'S REVIEW

Test Yourself

§1.

Pronunciation

Circle the letter of the correct answer.

1. The vowel *a* in the Japanese word *ame is* pronounced as in the English word
   A. lather   B. bather   C. ago   D. father

2. The vowel *i* in the Japanese word *imi* is pronounced like the vowel sound in the English word
   A. see   B. him   D. kite   E. mild

3. The vowel *o* in the Japanese word *otoko* is pronounced like the *o* in the English word
   A. not   B. bother   C. boat   D. reason

4. The vowel *u* in the Japanese word *uma is* pronounced like the *u* in the English word
   A. cup   B. cute   C. church   D. suit

5. The vowel *ei* in the Japanese word *eigo is* pronounced like the *e* in the following English word, but lengthened
   A. seen   B. river   C. begin   D. met

Match the Japanese words with their English meaning.

6. obasan _____   obāsan _____

7. ojisan _____   ojiisan _____

8. seki _____   seiki _____

   A. aunt   B. seat   C. grandfather
   D. century   E. grandmother   F. uncle

9. Kite kudasai. _____

10. Kitte kudasai. _____
    A. Please cut it.
    B. Please put it (clothing) on.

§2.

The Japanese
Writing System

Write the romaji and the English meaning for the Japanese words.

11. 山　　　　　_____ _____

12. 川　　　　　_____ _____

13. 日本　　　　_____ _____

14. 人　　　　　_____ , _____ _____

15. 日本人　　　_____ _____

Tell whether the following Japanese words are written in hiragana or katakana.

16. ひらがな　　_____

17. カタカナ　　　_____

18. スミス　　　　_____

19. さん　　　　　_____

20. ようこそ　　　_____

Word Order

In the following sentences the words are scrambled.
Rearrange them to form correct sentences.

21. sore o / shimashita / Jon san ga

_____

22. kaimashita / pan o / ka / okāsan ga

_____

23. otōsan ga / mimashita / eiga o / ka

_____

24. Nihonjin / Tanaka san wa / desu

_____

25. wa / takai / desu / kudamono

_____

26. hon / donna / sore wa / ka / desu

_____

§4.

Nouns

Circle the letter of the correct answer for each item.

27. Which of the following words should be capitalized?
    A. tanaka san   B. kinyōbi   C. rokugatsu

28. Which of the following languages should not be capitalized?
    A. Chūgokugo   B. Furansugo   C. Eigo
    D. Supeingo

Check the appropriate box for each Japanese sentence.

29. Tanaka san wa, koko ni imasu.
    Mr. Tanaka is here. ☐
    Mrs. Tanaka is here. ☐
    Miss Tanaka is here. ☐
    Ms. Tanaka is here. ☐
    Any or all of the above. ☐

30. Hon o motte imasu.
    I have a book. ☐
    I have some books. ☐
    I have the books. ☐
    I have books. ☐
    Any or all of the above. ☐

Fill in the form that the Japanese prefer for each name.

31. Ano hito no namae wa _____ desu.
    (Tomomi Nakamura)

32. Watakushi wa _____ desu.
    (John Smith)

Write the polite form for the following nouns:

33. namae   _____

34. sake   _____

35. furo   _____

36. hon   _____

For each noun, write the Japanese for the place or shop where it is sold.

37. niku   _____

38. kamera   _____

For each noun, write the Japanese for a person with expertise or special knowledge on that subject.

39. seiji   _____

40. geijutsu   _____

§5.

Pronouns

For each pair of sentences, choose the one that is preferable in Japanese.

41. (talking about yourself)
    A. Watakushi wa Nikkō ni ikitai desu.
    B. Nikkō ni ikitai desu.

42. (talking to Mr. Wakabayashi)
    A. Anata wa ogenki desu ka.
    B. Wakabayashi san wa ogenki desu ka.

43. (talking about Mrs. Hirota)
    A. Hirota san wa ashita kimasu.
    B. Kanojo wa ashita kimasu.

44. (talking about John)
    A. Ano hito wa Amerikajin desu.
    B. Kare wa Amerikajin desu.

Match each interrogative pronoun with its meaning.

45. A. dare   _____ ☐ how many
    B. nan, nani   _____ ☐ why
    C. ikutsu   _____ ☐ how much
    D. dō   _____ ☐ how
    E. ikura   _____ ☐ what
    F. donna   _____ ☐ what kind of
    G. dōshite   _____ ☐ who

Select the appropriate indefinite pronoun.

46. _____ kimashita.
    A. dokomo   B. dareka   C. dokoka

47. _____ kimasen deshita.
    A. daremo   B. dokomo   C. ikura

In the following word-search puzzle there are 12 demonstrative pronoun forms. One is circled. Try to find the rest.

48.

P	Q	S	M	I	H	S	N	B	V
I	K	O	R	E	V	O	A	J	O
Q	D	R	A	Z	C	N	U	I	X
A	R	E	S	A	S	O	N	N	A
P	H	K	K	M	I	U	O	N	P
B	L	S	O	C	H	I	R	A	Q
S	B	T	C	W	O	P	Y	S	I
D	A	C	H	I	R	A	I	O	K
W	N	R	I	P	Y	N	W	K	O
I	N	E	R	P	K	O	N	O	B
N	A	I	A	Q	Z	V	O	T	S

§6.

Particles

The following sentences contain slots for particles used with words or phrases. Fill them in.

49. Yamaguchi san _____ sensei desu.
    (topic marker)

50. Dare _____ kore o shimashita ka.
    (subject marker)

51. Senshū sono hon _____ yomimashita.
    (direct object marker)

52. Kodomo _____ gakkō wa koko desu.
    (possessive marker)

53. Amerika _____ tabemono wa, oishii desu.
    (noun modification).

54. Hon o watakushi _____ kudasai.
    (indirect object marker)

55. Ginza wa Tōkyō _____ arimasu. (location)

56. Ano hito wa Amerika _____ kaerimashita.
    (direction)

57. Kayōbi _____ sore o shimashō.
    (specific time)

58. Sore _____ desu ka. (limitation)

59. Takushī _____ ikimashita. (means)

60. Kōbe _____ ikimasu ka. (direction)

61. Kisha wa Kyōto _____ kimashita. (origin)

62. Yūgata _____ benkyō shimashita.
    (target time)

63. Gohan _____ suki desu. (including)

64. Jon san _____ Merī san ga kimashita.
    (complete listing)

65. Pan _____ gohan no hō ga suki desu.
    (comparison)

The following sentences contain slots for particles used with clauses. Fill them in from the particles listed below.

☐ to   ☐ node   ☐ kara   ☐ nagara   ☐ noni

66. Isogashii _____ ikemasen. (reason)

67. Aruki _____ hanashimashita.
    (simultaneous action)

68. Hashitta _____ tsukaremashita.
    (cause and effect)

69. Takai _____ kaimashita. (contrast)

70. Kangaeru _____ wakarimasu. (condition)

The following sentences contain slots for particles used at the end of sentences. Fill them in.

71. Imōto san wa sensei desu _____ .
    (question marker)

72. Atsui desu _____ . (confirmation)

73. Benkyō shinasai _____ . (emphatic)

74. Watakushi ga suru _____ .
    (female sentence ending)

§7.

Verbs

For the following c-stem verbs, the dictionary form is given. Per the example, give the stem and the infinitive.

75. DICTIONARY FORM STEM INFINITIVE

Example
isogu (to hurry) isog- isogi-

kaku (to write) _____ _____
nuru (to paint) _____ _____
tobu (to fly) _____ _____
shinu (to die) _____ _____
yomu (to read) _____ _____

For the following v-stem verbs, the dictionary form is given. Per the example, give the stem and the infinitive.

76. DICTIONARY FORM STEM INFINITIVE

Example
ageru (to give, to raise) age- age-

dekiru (to be able) _____ _____
hajimeru (to begin) _____ _____
iru (to be) _____ _____
kangaeru (to think) _____ _____
miru (to see) _____ _____

Fill in the correct past tense form of the verb *taberu*.

77. Ban gohan o _____ ato, terebi o mita.

78. Ban gohan o _____ ato, terebi o mimashita

Complete each sentence with a form of *desu, arimasu*, or *imasu*.

79. Kore wa hon _____ .

80. Tanaka san wa sensei _____ .

81. Kyō wa otenki ga ii _____ .

82. Ashita wa tabun otenki ga warui _____ .

83. Ano hito wa kinō byōki _____ .

84. Hon wa tēburu no ue ni _____ .

85. Okane ga arimasu ka. Iie, _____ .

86. Fujisan wa Nihon ni _____ .

87. Tanaka san wa _____ ka. Hai,
    _____ .

88. Ichimura san wa kinō Tōkyō ni _____ ka.

89. Sumisu san wa tabun raigetsu Nihon ni _____ .

Fill in the polite present tense form of the verb.

90. Watakushi wa kōhī o _____ .
    (nomu, negative)

91. Yamakawa san wa mainichi sushi o _____ .
    (taberu)

92. Ano hitotachi wa terebi o _____ .
    (miru, negative)

93. Nihongo ga _____ ka. (wakaru)

94. Ashita Kyōto ni _____ . (iku)

Fill in the polite past tense form of the verb.

95. Itsu _____ ka. (kuru)

96. Mada _____ . (suru, negative)

97. Gohan ga _____ . (owaru)

98. Doko de _____ ka. (kau)

99. Doko ni _____ ka. (iku)

Fill in the polite present progressive form of the verb.

100. Yamada san wa rajio o _____ .
     (kiku, negative)

101. Okada san wa hon o _____ .
     (yomu)

102. Doa ga _____ . (aku)

Fill in the polite past progressive form of the verb.

103. Kyonen Tōkyō de _____ .
     (hataraku)

104. Kinō haha wa _____ .
     (tsukareru, negative)

Fill in the polite presumptive form of the verb.

105. Ashita ame ga _____ .
     (furu, probability)

106. Rainen Nihon e _____ .
     (iku, intention)

Choose the form of the imperative which is the most polite.

107. A. Tabete kudasai.   B. Tabenasai.   C. Tabero.

Fill in two different potential forms in the sentences below.

108. Tanaka san wa, eigo ga _____ .
     (can speak)

109. Jon san wa, Nihongo ga _____ .
     (can do)

Fill in the passive form of the verb.

110. Sono hon wa kyonen _____ .
     (kaku)

111. Tarō san wa otōsan ni _____ .
     (shinu)

Adjectives

Choose the appropriate answer from the verbal adjectives below.

☐ oishii   ☐ hayai   ☐ muzukashii   ☐ kuroi

112. _____ kutsu o kaimasu.

113. Kinō _____ gohan o tabemashita.

114. _____ hon o yomimashita.

Fill in the polite verbal form of the verbal adjective.

115. Kono hon wa _____ . (is interesting)

116. Kisha wa _____ . (was fast)

117. Shiken wa _____ . (isn't easy)

Fill in the polite adverbial form of the verbal adjective.

118. Ichirō san wa _____ benkyō shimasu. (ii)

119. _____ tabemashita. (hayai)

120. Tenki ga _____ narimashita. (suzushii)

Fill in the form of the adjectival noun as a noun modifier.

121. _____ hana ga hoshii desu. (kirei)

122. Tanaka san wa _____ hito desu.
(shinsetsu)

123. Sore wa _____ kisha desu. (fuben)

Choose the appropriate answer from the adjectival nouns below.

☐ jōzu   ☐ iroiro   ☐ genki   ☐ benri

124. Yūko san wa supōtsu ga _____ desu.

125. Kono basu wa _____ deshita.

126. Mēri san wa _____ dewa arimasen.

Fill in the adverbial form of the adjectival noun.

127. Ichihashi san wa _____ arukimasu. (quietly)

128. Suzuki san wa eigo ga _____ narimashita. (good at)

129. Sumisu san wa _____ hanashimashita. (politely)

Fill in the word you need to make a comparison.

130. Banana wa budō _____ yasui desu.

131. Basu yori takushī no _____ benri desu.

§9.

Adverbs

Fill in the Japanese equivalent of the English adverb.

132. Eki wa _____ ni arimasu. (over there)

133. Misako san wa _____ benkyō shimasu. (every night)

134. Yūbin wa _____ desu. (yet, not yet)

135. _____ shite kudasai. (this way)

136. _____ kite kudasai. (tomorrow)

137. _____ shite kudasai. (quickly)

138. Satō san wa _____ hataraite imasu. (always)

139. Ban gohan wa _____ oishikatta desu. (very)

140. _____ matte kudasai. (a moment)

141. _____ hanashite kudasai. (slowly)

142. _____ arukimashō. (more)

143. Hon wa _____ omoshiroku arimasen deshita. (at all)

§10.

Numbers

Write two ways of saying each number in Japanese.

144. 3 _____ _____

145. 6 _____ _____

146. 10 _____ _____

Write out each number in words.

147. 17 _____

148. 81 _____

149. 600 _____

150. 7,000 _____

151. 10,000 _____

152. 200,000 _____

153. 1,000,000 _____

154. 100,000,000 _____

Write the Japanese words for the ordinal numbers.

155. fourth _____

156. ninth _____

§11.

Telling Time

Write in Japanese the time shown on each of the following clocks.

157. Nanji desu ka.

A.M.

A. _____   B. _____   C. _____

D. _____   E. _____   F. _____

P.M.

G. _____   H. _____   I. _____

J. _____   K. _____   L. _____

M. _____   N. _____   O. _____

§12.

Classifiers

Give the appropriate classifier for each item.

158. hon o _____ (5)

159. kōhī o _____ (3)

160. neko o _____ (4)

161. uchi o _____ (10)

162. ringo o _____ (7)

163. kami o _____ (2)

§13.

Days, Months, Seasons, and the Weather

Write the days of the week in the crossword puzzle.

164. ACROSS

1. Saturday
3. Tuesday
5. Wednesday
7. Monday

DOWN

2. Sunday
4. Friday
6. Thursday

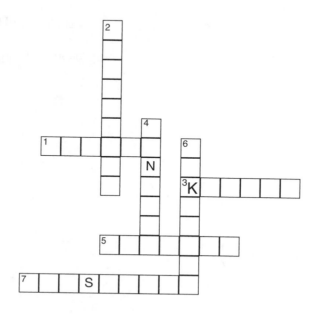

Fill in the blanks in the sentences below.

165. _____ kyōto ni ikimasu. (next week)

166. Kono _____ aimashō. (weekend)

167. Watakushi no tanjōbi wa _____ desu. (April)

168. _____ wa gakkō ga yasumi desu. (the 7th)

169. Watakushi wa _____ byōki deshita. (last month)

How's the weather? Write the appropriate Japanese response in each sentence below.

170. _____ tenki desu. (beautiful)

171. _____ imasu. (raining)

172. _____ desu. (hot and humid)

173. _____ imasu. (snowing)

§14.

Family Relationships

You're talking about your own family. Match the Japanese word with its English equivalent.

174. haha	☐ daughter
175. musume	☐ wife
176. tsuma	☐ mother
177. sobo	☐ elder sister
178. ane	☐ grandmother

Now you're talking about someone else's family. Match the Japanese word with its English equivalent.

179. goshujin	☐ daughter
180. otōsan	☐ cousin
181. ojōsan	☐ husband
182. otōtosan	☐ younger brother
183. itoko	☐ father

§15.

Useful Words and Phrases

Fill in the Japanese greeting appropriate for the time of day.

184. _____. (9 A.M.)

185. _____. (2 P.M.)

186. _____. (8 P.M.)

Complete the useful expressions below by supplying the missing Japanese.

187. _____ ga. (Pardon me, but ....)

188. _____ matte kudasai.
     (Just a moment, please.)

189. Mō sukoshi _____.
     (Please speak slowly.)

Can you describe your personal condition?
Fill in the Japanese.

190. _____ imasu. (I'm thirsty.)

191. _____ imasu. (I'm tired.)

192. _____ desu. (I'm sick.)

Introductions are important in Japan! Write the missing words below.

193. Ano kata ni _____ no desu ga.
     (I would like to meet him/her.)

194. Ano kata ni shōkai shite _____ ka.
     (Would you introduce me to him/her?)

195. _____ o dōzo.
     (Here's my card.)

§16.

Borrowed Words

For each Japanese word borrowed from English, choose the meaning.

196. pasokon
    A. convenience store   B. convenient pass
    C. personal computer   D. personal convenience

197. depāto
    A. department store   B. department
    C. departure   D. departure lounge

198. basuke
    A. basket   B. basketball
    C. bask   D. bus ticket

199. baikingu
    A. bicycling   B. baked goods
    C. baking school   D. smorgasbord

200. manshon
    A. man-made   B. large house
    C. estate   D. condo

§17.

Synonyms

Replace the underlined word with a new one that doesn't change the meaning of the sentence.

201. Tanaka san wa <u>chūshoku</u> o tabemasen deshita.

202. Okāsan wa <u>yakkyoku</u> ni ikimashita.

203. <u>Kūkō</u> made densha de ikimashita.

204. Tanaka san wa <u>yōshoku</u> ga suki desu.

205. <u>Toire</u> wa doko ni arimasu ka.

206. Suzuki san wa <u>yashashii</u> desu.

Choose the word that has the same meaning.

207. depāto
   - A. shoten
   - B. yokushitsu
   - C. hyakkaten
   - D. honya

208. kireina
   - A. okashina
   - B. shinsetsuna
   - C. shizukana
   - D. utsukushii

209. tadachi ni
   - A. hijō ni
   - B. sugu ni
   - C. shizuka ni
   - D. muzukashii

210. shigoto suru
   - A. seiton suru
   - B. shippai suru
   - C. rikai suru
   - D. hataraku

§18.

Antonyms

Match the words that have opposite meanings.

211. jōzu   A. owaru

212. noru   B. kurai

213. takai   C. oriru

214. hajimaru   D. osoi

215. yasashii   E. hikui

216. akarui   F. heta

217. shizukana   G. chigau

218. takai   H. muzukashii

219. onaji   I. yasui

220. hayai   J. urusai

§19.

Short Vowel, Long Vowel

Fill in the proper word.

221. a new student   atarashii _____

222. big figures   ōkii _____

223. difficult situations   muzukashii _____

224. a courageous person   _____ ga aru hito

225. going out at 4 o'clock   _____ ni dekakeru

226. an interesting plot   omoshiroi _____

227. a kind woman   shinsetsuna _____

228. new information   atarashii _____

229. returning to one's hometown _____ ni kaeru

230. important business   taisetsuna _____

§20.

Double Consonants

Choose the correct word for each sentence.

231. Musume wa mainichi (niki / nikki) o kakimasu.

232. Nihon no kaisha ga Amerikajin o (boshū shite / bosshū shite) imasu.

233. Kobe niwa (saka / sakka) ga takusan arimasu.

234. Depāto de (shoki / shokki) o kaimashita.

235. Mizu ga (futō / futtō) shite imasu.

§21.

Same Pronunciation, Different Meaning

Which is the correct meaning?

236. <u>Kaze</u> ga tsuyoi desu. (wind / cold)

237. <u>Ha</u> ga itai desu. (tooth / leaf)

238. Kireina <u>hana</u> o kaimashita. (flower / nose)

239. Yamada san wa omoshiroi <u>kiji</u> o yomimashita. (article / cloth)

240. Ōkii <u>kumo</u> ga nihiki imasu. (cloud / spider)

§22.

Pitch Accent: Different Pitch, Different Meaning

Which underlined words have a high-pitched syllable (H)?
Which ones don't (L)?

241. <u>ame</u> o taberu　　( )

242. <u>ame</u> ga furu　　( )

243. <u>sake</u> o nomu　　( )

244. <u>sake</u> o taberu　　( )

245. kami o <u>kiru</u>　　( )

246. sētā o <u>kiru</u>　　( )

247. <u>ima</u> iku　　( )

248. <u>hashi</u> de taberu　　( )

249. kuruma o <u>kau</u>　　( )

250. <u>kisha</u> ni noru　　( )

Answers

§1.

Pronunciation

1–8 (see §1.2)

1. D. father

2. A. see

3. C. boat

4. D. suit

5. D. met

6. A. aunt, E. grandmother

7. F. uncle, C. grandfather

8. B. seat, D. century

9–10 (see §1.3)

9. B. Please put it (clothing) on.

10. A. Please cut it.

§2.

The Japanese Writing System

11–15 (see §2.2)

11. yama, mountain

12. kawa, river

13. Nihon, Japan

14. hito, jin, person

15. Nihonjin, Japanese

16–20 (see §2.3)

16. hiragana

17. katakana

18. katakana

19. hiragana

20. hiragana

§3.

Word Order

21–23 (see §3.3–1)

21. Jon san ga sore o shimashita.

22. Okāsan ga pan o kaimashita ka.

23. Otōsan ga eiga o mimashita ka.

24–26 (see §3.3–2)

24. Tanaka san wa Nihonjin desu.

25. Kudamono wa takai desu.

26. Sore wa donna hon desu ka.

§4.

Nouns

27–28 (see §4.1)

27. A. Tanaka san

28. C. eigo

29. (see §4.2) Any or all of the above.

30. (see §4.4) Any or all of the above.

31–32 (see §4.5 and §4.6)

31. Nakamura Tomomi

32. Jon Sumisu

33–36 (see §4.7)

33. onamae

34. osake

35. ofuro

36. gohon

37–40 (see §4.9)

37. nikuya

38. kameraya

39. seijika

40. geijutsuka

§5.

Pronouns

41. (see §5.2) B. Nikkō ni ikitai desu.

42–44 (see §5.2–1)

42. B. Wakabayashi san wa ogenki desu ka.

43. A. Hirota san wa ashita kimasu.

44. A. Ano hito wa Amerikajin desu.

45. (see §5.3) A. dare–who; B. nan, nani–what;
C. ikutsu–how many; D. dō–how; E. ikura–how much;
F. donna–what kind of; G. dōshite–why

46–47 (see §5.4)

46. B. dareka

47. A. daremo

48. (see §5.5)

P	Q	S	M	I	H	S	N	B	V
I	K	O	R	E	V	O	A	J	O
Q	D	R	A	Z	C	N	U	I	X
A	R	E	S	A	S	O	N	N	A
P	H	K	K	M	I	U	O	N	P
B	L	S	O	C	H	I	R	A	Q
S	B	T	C	W	O	P	Y	S	I
D	A	C	H	I	R	A	I	O	K
W	N	R	I	P	Y	N	W	K	O
I	N	E	R	P	K	O	N	O	B
N	A	I	A	Q	Z	V	O	T	S

§6.

Particles

§7.

Verbs

75–76 (see §7.3 1, §7.3 2, and §7.4)

75. kak-, kaki-; nur-, nuri-; tob-, tobi-; shin-, shini-; yom-, yomi-

76. deki-, deki-; hajime-, hajime-; i-, i-; kangae-, kangae-; mi-, mi-

77–78 (see §7.5)

77. tabeta

78. tabeta

79–89 (see §7.6)

79. desu

80. desu

81. desu

82. deshō

83. deshita

84. arimasu

85. arimasen

86. arimasu

87. imasu, imasu

88. imashita

89. iru deshō

90–94 (see §7.7–1)

90. nomimasen

91. tabemasu

92. mimasen

93. wakarimasu

94. ikimasu

95–99 (see §7.7–2)

95. kimashita

96. shimasen deshita

97. owarimashita

98. kaimashita

99. ikimashita

100–102 (see §7.7–4)

100. kiite imasen

101. yonde imasu

102. aite imasu

103–104 (see §7.7–5)

103. hataraite imashita

104. tsukarete imasen deshita

105–106 (see §7.8)

105. furu deshō

106. iku deshō

107. (see §7.9) A. Tabete kudasai.

108–109 (see §7.11)

108. hanasemasu

109. dekimasu

110–111 (see §7.12)

110. kakaremashita

111. shinaremashita

§8.

Adjectives

§9.

Adverbs

132. (see §9.2) asoko

133–134 (see §9.3)

133. maiban

134. mada

135–143 (see §9.4)

135. kō

136. Ashita

137. Isoide

138. itsumo

139. totemo

140. Chotto

141. Yukkuri

142. Motto

143. zenzen

§10.

Numbers

144–154 (see § 10.1)

144. san; mittsu

145. roku; muttsu

146. jū; tō

147. jūshichi; jūnana

148. hachijūichi

149. roppyaku

150. nanasen

151. ichiman

152. nijūman

153. hyakuman

154. ichioku

155–156 (see §10.2)

155. yonbanme

156. kyūbanme

§11.

Telling Time

157. (see §11)

A. Niji desu.

B. Niji han desu.

C. Goji juppun mae desu.

D. Jūji yonjuppun desu.

E. Kuji jūgofun desu.

F. Jūji yonjūgofun desu. or
Jūichiji jūgofun mae desu.

G. Hachiji yonjuppun desu.

H. Rokuji han desu.

I. Shichiji jūgofun desu.

J. Sanji desu.

K. Yoji yonjuppun desu.

L. Jūji gofun mae desu.

M. Kuji han desu.

N. Jūichiji yonjūgofun desu. or Jūniji jūgofun
mae desu.

O. Jūniji desu.

§12.

Classifiers

158–163 (see §12)

158. gosatsu

159. sanbai

160. yonhiki

161. jukken

162. nanako; nanatsu

163. nimai

§13.

Days, Months, Seasons, and the Weather

164–166 (see §13.1)

164.

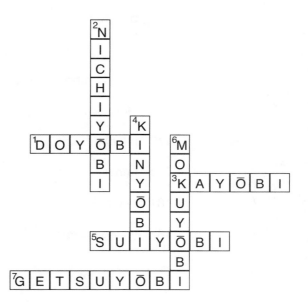

165. Raishū

166. shūmatsu

167. (see §13.2) shigatsu

168. (see § 13.3) Nanoka

169. (see §13.4) sengetsu

170–173 (see § 13.6)

170. Ii

171. Ame ga futte

172. Mushiatsui

173. Yuki ga futte

§14.

Family Relationships

174–183 (see §14)

174. mother

175. daughter

176. wife

177. grandmother

178. elder sister

179. husband

180. father

181. daughter

182. younger brother

183. cousin

§15.

Useful Words and Phrases

184–186 (see §15.1)

184. Ohayō gozaimasu.

185. Konnichiwa.

186. Konbanwa.

187–189 (see §15.2)

187. Sumimasen

188. Chotto

189. yukkuri hanashite kudasai.

190–192 (see §15.4)

190. Nodo ga kawaite

191. Tsukarete

192. Byōki

193–195 (see §15.5)

193. ome ni kakaritai

194. itadakemasen

195. Meishi

§16.

Borrowed Words

196–200 (see §16)

196. C. personal computer

197. A. department store

198. B. basketball

199. D. smorgasbord

200. D. condo

§17.

Synonyms

201–210 (see §17)

201. hirugohan

202. kusuriya

203. hikōjō

204. seiyō ryōri

205. otearai

206. shinsetsu

207. C. hyakkaten

208. D. utsukushii

209. B. sugu ni

210. D. hataraku

§18.

Antonyms

211. F. heta

212. C. oriru

213. E. hikui

214. A. owaru

215. H. muzukashii

216. B. kurai

217. J. urusai

218. I. yasui

219. G. chigau

220. D. osoi

§19.

Short Vowel, Long Vowel

221–230 (see §19)

221. seito

222. sūji

223. jōshei

224. yūki

225. yoji

226. suji

227. josei

228. jōhō

229. kokyō

230. yōji

§20.

Double Consonants

§21.

Same Pronunciation, Different Meaning

236–240 (see §21)

236. wind

237. tooth

238. flower

239. article

240. spider

§22.

Pitch Accent: Different Pitch, Different Meaning

241–250 (see §22)

241. ame   L

242. ame   H

243. sake   L

244. sake   H

245. kiru   L

246. kiru   H

247. ima   H

248. hashi   H

249. kau   L

250. kasha   L

Japanese-English Vocabulary

Abbreviations: (adj.) adjective; (adv.) adverb; (conj.) conjunction; (excl.) exclamation; (n.) noun; (p.) particle; (ph.) phrase; (pron.) pronoun; (v.) verb.

ā (adv.), (pron.) **in that manner, like that, that way**
achira (adv.), (pron.) **there, that**
ageru (v.) **to give**
ageru (v.) **to raise**
aisatsu (n.) **greeting**
akai (adj.) **red**
akarui (adj.) **bright**
aki (n.) **autumn**
aku (v.) **to open**
amai (adj.) **sweet**
amari (adv.) **not much, not often**
ame (n.) **rain**
ame (n.) **candy**
amu (v.) **to knit**
anata (pron.) **you**
anatagata (pron.) **you (polite)**
anatatachi (pron.) **you (plural)**
ane (n.) **elder sister (one's own)**
anna (adj.) **that kind of**
ano (adj.) **that**
ano hito (ph.) **that person**
ano hitotachi (ph.) **those persons**
ano kata (ph.) **that person (polite)**
ano katatachi (ph.) **those persons (polite)**
apāto (n.) **apartment**
arau (v.) **to wash**
are (pron.) **that**
aru (v.) **(there) is/are, to be located, to exist, to have**
aruku (v.) **to walk**
asa (n.) **morning**
asagohan (n.) **breakfast**
asatte (n.) **the day after tomorrow**

ashi (n.) **foot**
ashita (adv.), (n.) **tomorrow**
asobu (v.) **to play**
asoko (adv.), (pron.) **over there**
atama (n.) **head**
atarashii (adj.) **new**
ato (n.) **after, the following**
atsui (adj.) **hot**
atsui (adj.) **thick**
au (v.) **to meet, to see**

bakari, bakkari (adv.) **only**
banana (n.) **banana**
bangohan (n.) **dinner**
basu (n.) **bus**
batā (n.) **butter**
benkyō suru (v.) **to study**
benri (adj.) **convenient**
betsu no (adj.) **different**
biru (n.) **building**
bōeki gaisha (n.) **trading company**
bōnasu (n.) **bonus**
budō (n.) **grapes**
byōki (n.) **illness, sickness**

chichi (n.) **father (one's own)**
chigatta (adj.) **different**
chigau (adj.) **different**
chiisai (adj.) **small**
chikatetsu (n.) **subway**
chizu (n.) **map**
chōshoku (n.) **breakfast**
chotto (adv.) **a little, for a moment**
Chūgokugo (n.) **Chinese (language)**
chūshoku (n.) **lunch**

245

da (v.) **to be, plain form of desu**
daidokoro (n.) **kitchen**
dakedo (conj.) **but**
dame (adj.) **no good**
dandan (adv.) **gradually**
dare (pron.) **who**
dareka (pron.) **someone**
daremo (pron.) **no one**
dasu (v.) **to take out**
de (p.) **among, at, from, made from, made of, of, within**
dekakeru (v.) **to go out**
dekiru (v.) **to be able**
denki (n.) **light**
denwa suru (v.) **to telephone**
depāto (n.) **department store**
deru (v.) **to depart**
desu (v.) **is, are**
dō (adv.), (pron.) **how**
doa (n.) **door**
dochira (pron.) **where, which (direction, preference)**
dōgu (n.) **tool**
Doitsugo (n.) **German (language)**
doko (pron.) **where (place)**
dokoka (pron.) **somewhere**
dokomo (pron.) **nowhere**
donata (pron.) **which person (polite)**
donataka (pron.) **someone (polite)**
donatamo (pron.) **no one (polite)**
donna (pron.), (adj.) **what kind of**
dore (pron.) **which (persons, things)**
doreka (pron.) **something**
doremo (pron.) **nothing**
dōro (n.) **road**
dōshite (pron.) **why**
doyōbi (n.) **Saturday**

e (p.) **to, toward**
ebi (n.) **shrimp**
eiga (n.) **movie**
eigo (n.) **English**
eki (n.) **station**
enpitsu (n.) **pencil**

fuben (adj.) **inconvenient**
Fujisan (n.) **Mt. Fuji**

Furansugo (n.) **French (language)**
furo (n.) **bath**
furoba (n.) **bathroom**
furu (v.) **to fall (rain, snow, etc.)**
futoi (adj.) **thick**
futoru (v.) **to get fat**
futsū (adv.) **usually**
futtō (n.) **boiling**
fuyu (n.) **winter**

ga (p.) **and**
ga (p.) **although, but**
ga (p.) **subject marker**
gakkō (n.) **school**
ganbaru (v.) **to try hard**
geijutsu (n.) **art**
geijutsuka (n.) **artist**
gēmu (n.) **game**
genki (adj.) **healthy, well**
getsuyōbi (n.) **Monday**
gin (n.) **silver**
gogo (n.) **afternoon**
gohan (n.) **cooked rice, meal**
gohon (n.) **book (polite)**
goi (n.) **vocabulary**
gokekkon (n.) **marriage (polite)**
gozen (n.) **(in the) morning**

ha (n.) **tooth**
hahaoya (n.) **mother, mothers**
hahaoyatachi (n.) **mothers**
hairu (v.) **to enter**
hajimaru (v.) **to begin**
hajime (n.) **beginning**
hajimeru (v.) **to begin**
han (n.) **half past**
hana (n.) **flower**
hana (n.) **nose**
hanasu (v.) **to speak, to talk**
harau (v.) **to pay**
haru (n.) **spring**
hashi (n.) **chopsticks**
hashi (n.) **bridge**
hashiru (v.) **to run**
hataraku (v.) **to work**
hayai (adj.) **early, fast, quick**
hayaku (adv.) **early, quick, quickly**

henna (adj.) **strange**
heta (n.), (adj.) **bad at**
heta (n.), (adj.) **poor at**
heya (n.) **room**
hi (n.) **day**
hijō ni (adv.) **very**
hikōjō (n.) **airport**
hikui (adj.) **low**
hiragana (n.) *hiragana*, **one kind of Japanese syllabary**
hiroi (adj.) **spacious**
hirugohan (n.) **lunch**
hito (n.) **person**
hitsuyō (n.) **need**
hodo (p.) **as . . . as, as much as**
hōmon suru (v.) **to visit**
hon (n.) **book**
honya (n.) **bookstore, bookstore clerk, bookstore owner**
hoshii (adj.) **need, want**
hosoi (adj.) **thin**
hoteru (n.) **hotel**
hotondo (adv.) **all but, almost, hardly**
hyakkaten (n.) **department store**
hyōron (n.) **commentary**
hyōronka (n.) **critic**

ichiban (adv.), (n.) **the best, most**
ie (n.) **house, home**
ii (adj.) **good, nice, okay**
iiharu (v.) **to insist**
ikaga (adv.) **how, how about?, would you like?**
ikeru (v.) **can go**
iku (v.) **to go**
ikura (pron.) **how much**
ikuraka (pron.) **some, a little**
ikuramo (pron.) **not much**
ikutsu (pron.) **how many**
ima (adv.), (n.) **now**
ima (n.) **living room**
imi (n.) **meaning**
imōto (n.) **younger sister**
inu (n.) **dog**
iroiro (adj.) **various**

iru (v.) **to need**
iru (v.) **to be, to exist**
isogashii (adj.) **busy**
isogu (v.) **to hurry**
issho ni (adv.) **together**
isshōkenmei (adv.) **hard**
isu (n.) **chair**
itadaku (v.) **to receive (from superiors)**
itai (adj.) **painful**
itsu (pron.) **when**
itsuka (pron.) **sometime**
itsumo (adv.), (pron.) **always**
iu (v.) **to say**

ji (n.) **o'clock**
jidōsha **car**
jikan (n.) **time**
jōgi (n.) **ruler**
josei (n.) **woman**
jōsei (n.) **situation**
joyū (n.) **actress**
jōzu (n.), (adj.) **good at**

ka (p.) **question marker**
ka (p.) **or**
kado (n.) **corner**
kaeru (v.) **to change**
kaeru (v.) **to return**
kaimono (n.) **shopping**
kaisha (n.) **company**
kaku (v.) **to write**
kamera (n.) **camera**
kameraya (n.) **camera shop, camera shop owner, camera shop clerk**
kami (n.) **paper**
kamu (v.) **to bite**
kan (n.) **period**
Kanada (n.) **Canada**
kane (n.) **money**
kanemochi (n.) **rich person**
kangaeru (v.) **to think**
kanji (n.) *kanji*, **Chinese characters**
kankō (n.) **tour, sightseeing**
kanojo (pron.) **she, her**
kanojora (pron.) **they, them (female)**

kanojotachi (pron.) **they, them (female)**
kara (p.) **from**
kara (p.) **because, since**
kara (p.) **after, ever since, since**
kare (pron.) **he, him**
karera (pron.) **they, them (all male or male and female)**
kariru (v.) **to borrow**
karui (adj.) **light**
kasa (n.) **umbrella**
kashu (n.) **singer**
kasu (v.) **to lend**
katai (adj.) **hard**
katakana (n.) *katakana*, **one kind of Japanese syllabary**
kau (v.) **to buy**
kau (v.) **to keep (a pet)**
kawa (n.) **river**
kayōbi (n.) **Tuesday**
kaze (n.) **wind**
kaze (n.) **cold**
keikan (n.) **police officer**
kēki (n.) **cake**
kekkon (n.) **marriage**
kekkon suru (v.) **to get married**
keredo (p.) **and**
keredo (p.) **although, but, however**
keredomo (conj.) **but**
kesu (v.) **to turn off**
ki (n.) **tree, wood**
ki o tsukeru (v.) **to be careful**
kiiroi (adj.) **yellow**
kiji (n.) **article**
kiji (n.) **cloth**
kiku (v.) **to hear, to listen, to ask**
kimochi (n.) **feeling**
kinō (adv.), (n.) **yesterday**
kinyōbi (n.) **Friday**
kirei (adj.) **beautiful**
kiru (v.) **to put on (clothing)**
kiru (v.) **to cut**
kisha (n.) **train**
kisha (n.) **reporter**
kitto (adv.) **certainly, surely**
kō (adv.), (pron.) **in this manner, like this, this way**

kōcha (n.) **tea**
kochira (adv.), (pron.) **here, this**
kodomo (n.) **child, children**
kodomotachi (n.) **children**
kōen (n.) **park**
kōhī (n.) **coffee**
koko (adv.), (pron.) **here**
kokoa (n.) **cocoa**
kokyō (n.) **hometown**
kōkyō (n.) **public**
komu (v.) **to be crowded**
kondo (n.) **this time**
konna (adj.) **this kind of**
kono (adj.) **this, these**
konshū (n.) **this week**
konzatsu suru (v.) **to be crowded**
kore (pron.) **this**
koshikake (n.) **chair**
koshō (n.) **breakdown**
kōto (n.) **coat**
kotoshi (n.) **this year**
kudamono (n.) **fruit**
kudaru (v.) **to descend**
kudasai (v.) **to give (me), please**
kudasaru (v.) **to give kindly (to me or my in-group) (polite)**
kūki (n.) **air**
kukkī (n.) **cookie**
kūkō (n.) **airport**
kumo (n.) **spider**
kumo (n.) **cloud**
kumoru (v.) **to get clouded**
kuni (n.) **country**
kurai (adj.) **dark**
kurasu (n.) **class**
kureru (v.) **to give kindly (to me or my in-group)**
kuroi (adj.) **black**
kuru (v.) **to come**
kuruma (n.) **car**
kusuriya (n.) **pharmacy**
kutsu (n.) **shoes**
kyō (adv.), (n.) **today**
kyōkasho (n.) **textbook**
kyonen (n.) **last year**

machi (n.) **town**
mada (adv.) **(not) yet, still**
made (p.) **as far as, until**
made ni (p.) **by, no later than**
mado (n.) **window**
mae (adv.), (n.) **before**
maiasa (adv.), (n.) **every morning**
maiban (adv.), (n.) **every night**
mainichi (adv.), (n.) **every day**
makeru (v.) **to discount**
mata (adv.) **again**
matsu (v.) **to wait**
me (n.) **eye**
meron (n.) **melon**
michi (n.) **road, street**
mijikai (adj.) **short**
minasama (n.) **everyone, you all
(very polite)**
minasan (n.) **everyone, you all (polite)**
minna (adv.), (n.) **all, everyone, you all**
miru (v.) **to see, to watch**
miruku (n.) **milk**
mise (n.) **store**
mo (p.) **also, too**
mo (p.) **(not) either, neither. . . nor**
mo (p.) **even**
mō (adv.) **already, more**
modoru (v.) **to return**
mokuyōbi (n.) **Thursday**
momo (n.) **peach**
mono (n.) **thing**
morau (v.) **to receive**
motsu (v.) **to hold**
motto (adv.) **more, much more**
muryō no (adj.) **free**
muzukashii (adj.) **difficult**

nagai (adj.) **long**
nagara (p.) **as, while**
nakanaka (adv.) **at all, completely,
quite, rather**
naku (v.) **to cry**
nakusu (v.) **to lose**
namae (n.) **name**
nan (pron.) **what**
nandemo (pron.) **anything**

nani (pron.) **what**
nanika (pron.) **something**
nanimo, nannimo (pron.) **nothing**
nannin (pron.) **how many people**
naosu (v.) **to fix**
naru (v.) **to become**
natsu (n.) **summer**
naze (adv.) **why**
ne (p.) **Don't you think so?, Isn't it?**
nedan (n.) **price**
neko (n.) **cat**
nekutai (n.) **necktie**
nemui (adj.) **sleepy**
neru (v.) **to sleep**
neteshimau (v.) **to fall asleep**
ni tsuite (ph.) **about**
ni (p.) **on, to**
nichiyōbi (n.) **Sunday**
Nihon (n.) **Japan**
Nihongo (n.) **Japanese (language)**
Nihonjin (n.) **Japanese**
Nihon ryōri (n.) **Japanese food**
nikki (n.) **diary**
niku (n.) **meat**
nikuya (n.) **butcher, butcher shop**
no (p.) **posessive marker**
noboru (v.) **to climb**
node (p.) **because, since**
nomu (v.) **to drink**
noni (p.) **although, in spite of**
noru (v.) **to get on**
nōto (n.) **notebook**
nugu (v.) **to take off**
nuru (v.) **to paint**
nusumu (v.) **to steal**

o (p.) **object marker**
obasan (n.) **aunt (someone else's)**
obāsan (n.) **grandmother (someone
else's)**
oboeru (v.) **to learn**
ocha (n.) **Japanese tea**
ofuro (n.) **bath (polite)**
ohashi (n.) **chopsticks (polite)**
ohayō gozaimasu (ph.) **Good
morning (polite)**

ohayō (excl.) **Good morning**
oikakeru (v.) **to chase**
oishii (adj.) **delicious**
ojiisan (n.) **grandfather (someone else's)**
ojisan (n.) **uncle (someone else's)**
okane (n.) **money (polite)**
okāsan (n.) **mother (someone else's)**
okashina (adj.) **strange**
okatte (n.) **kitchen**
ōkii (adj.) **big**
omochi suru (v.) **to bring (polite)**
omoi (adj.) **heavy**
omoshiroi (adj.) **good, interesting**
omou (v.) **to think**
onaji (adj.) **same**
onamae (n.) **name (polite)**
oniku (n.) **meat (polite)**
onnanoko (n.) **girl, girls**
onnanokotachi (n.) **girls**
orenji (n.) **orange**
oriru (v.) **to get off**
osake (n.) **sake, rice wine (polite)**
ōsama (n.) **king**
oshieru (v.) **to teach**
osoi (adj.) **slow**
otearai (n.) **toilet**
otegami (n.) **letter (polite)**
otenki (n.) **weather (polite)**
otoko (n.) **male**
otokonoko (n.) **boy, boys**
otokonokotachi (n.) **boys**
otōsan (n.) **father (someone else's)**
otōto (n.) **younger brother**
ototoi (n.) **the day before yesterday**
owari (n.) **ending**
owaru (v.) **to finish**
oyasai (n.) **vegetables (polite)**
oyogu (v.) **to swim**

pan (n.) **bread**
purezento (n.) **gift**

raigetsu (n.) **next month**
raishū (n.) **next week**
reinkōto (n.) **raincoat**
reji (n.) **cashier**

rekishi (n.) **history**
rekōdo (n.) **record**
resutoran (n.) **restaurant**
rikai suru (v.) **to understand**
ringo (n.) **apple**
rippa (adj.) **gorgeous**
rokugatsu (n.) **June**
rōmaji (n.) *romaji*, **roman letters**
ryokō (n.) **trip**
ryōri (n.) **cooking**

saifu (n.) **wallet**
saigo (n.) **ending**
saikin (adv.) **recently**
saisho (n.) **beginning**
saka (n.) **slope**
sakana (n.) **fish**
sake (n.) *sake*, **rice wine**
sake (n.) **salmon**
sakka (n.) **writer**
samui (adj.) **cold (weather)**
san (n.) **Mr., Mrs., Miss, Ms.**
sangatsu (n.) **March**
sashiageru (v.) **to give (to superiors)**
sashimi (n.) *sashimi*, **raw fish**
satō (n.) **sugar**
seiji (n.) **politics**
seijika (n.) **politician**
seiki (n.) **century**
seito (n.) **student**
seitō (n.) **political party**
seiyō ryōri **western food**
seki (n.) **seat**
seki (n.) **cough**
sensei (n.) **teacher, teachers**
senseitachi (n.) **teachers**
senshu (n.) **player**
sensō (n.) **war**
sētā (n.) **sweater**
shachō (n.) **company president**
shiawase (adj.), (n.) **happy, happiness**
shigoto (n.) **work**
shigoto suru (v.) **to work**
shika (p.) **just, only**
shiken (n.) **exam**
shimaru (v.) **to close**

imau (v.) **to put away**
inbun (n.) **newspaper**
inpai suru (v.) **to worry**
insetsu (adj.) **kind**
insetsu ni (adv.) **kindly**
inu (v.) **to die**
iroi (adj.) **white**
iru (v.) **to know**
izuka (adj.) **quiet**
izuka ni (adv.) **quiet, quietly**
ōjiki (adj.) **honest**
okki (n.) **tableware**
ōsetsu (n.) **novel**
ōsetsuka (n.) **novelist**
oten (n.) **bookstore**
ū (n.) **week**
ūmatsu (n.) **weekend**
uppatsu suru (v.) **to depart**
(adv.), (pron.) **in that manner, like that, that way**
chira (adv.), (pron.) **there, that**
ko (adv.), (pron.) **there**
nna (adj.) **that kind of**
no (adj.) **that**
re (pron.) **it, that**
tto (adv.) **quietly**
barashii (adj.) **wonderful**
gi (adv.), (n.) **after, past**
gu (adv.) **immediately**
iyōbi (n.) **Wednesday**
ii (n.) **figure**
ii (n.) **plot**
ki (adj.) **to like**
kiyaki (n.) *sukiyaki*
koshi (adv.) **a little, few**
mu (v.) **to live**
pā (n.) **supermarket**
pōtsu (n.) **sports**
ru (v.) **to do**
rudoi (adj.) **sharp**
shi (n.) *sushi*
waru (v.) **to sit down**
zushii (adj.) **cool**

emono (n.) **food**
eru (v.) **to eat**

tabi (n.) **trip, travel**
tabitabi (adv.) **often**
tabun (adv.) **maybe, perhaps, probably**
tachi (suffix) **plural marker**
tada no (adj.) **free**
tadachi ni (adv.) **immediately**
taihen (adj.), (n.) **awful, bad**
taihen (adv.) **greatly, very (extreme degree, positive or negative)**
taisetsu (n.) **importance**
taitei (adv.) **generally, mainly, perhaps, probably**
takai (adj.) **expensive, high**
takusan (adv.) **a lot, many**
takushī (n.) **taxi**
tamani (adv.) **occasionally**
tara (adv.) **if, when**
tasu (v.) **to add**
tatsu (v.) **to stand**
te (n.) **hand**
tēburu (n.) **table**
tegami (n.) **letter**
teinei (adj.) **polite**
tenisu (n.) **tennis**
tenki (n.) **weather**
terebi (n.) **TV**
to (p.) **together with**
to (p.) **if, when**
to (p.) **and**
tobu (v.) **to fly**
tōchaku suru (v.) **to arrive**
toire (n.) **toilet**
toki (n.) **time**
tokidoki (adv.) **sometimes**
tokoro (n.) **place**
tomaru (v.) **to stop**
tomaru (v.) **to stay (overnight)**
toru (v.) **to take**
tōru (v.) **to go through**
toshi (n.) **year**
tōshi (n.) **investment**
toshokan (n.) **library**
totemo (adv.) **very**
tsugi (n.) **next**
tsukareru (v.) **to get tired**
tsukeru (v.) **to turn on**

tsuki (n.) **month**
tsuku (v.) **to arrive**
tsukuru (v.) **to make**
tsumetai (adj.) **cold**

uchi (n.) **home, house**
ue (n.) **top**
uma (n.) **horse**
umi (n.) **beach, sea**
untenshu (n.) **driver**
ureshii (adj.) **glad**
urusai (adj.) **noisy**
usui (adj.) **thin**
utsukushii (adj.) **beautiful**

wa (p.) **topic marker**
wa (p.) **(emphatic and softening
  effect)**
wakai (adj.) **young**
wakaru (v.) **understand**
warau (v.) **to laugh**
waribiku (v.) **to discount**
warui (adj.) **bad**
waruku (adv.) **bad, badly**
washoku (n.) **Japanese food**
watakushi (pron.) **I, me**
watakushitachi (pron.) **we, us**

ya (p.) **and**
yachin (n.) **rent**
yagate (adv.) **soon**
yakkyoku (n.) **pharmacy**
yakyū (n.) **baseball**
yama (n.) **mountain**

yasai (n.) **vegetables**
yasashii (adj.) **easy**
yasashii (adj.) **kind**
yaseru (v.) **to get thin**
yasui (adj.) **cheap**
yasumu (v.) **to rest**
yawarakai (adj.) **soft**
yo (p.) **(emphatic)**
yobu (v.) **to call**
yōji (n.) **business**
yoji (n.) **four o'clock**
yōkoso (excl.) **welcome**
yokushitsu (n.) **bathroom**
yoku (adv.) **better, much, often, well**
yomu (v.) **to read**
yori (p.) **than**
yorokobu (v.) **to be pleased**
yoru (n.) **night**
yōshoku **western food**
yotto (n.) **sailboat**
yūbin (n.) **mail**
yūbinkyoku (n.) **post office**
yūgata (n.) **evening**
yuki (n.) **snow**
yūki (n.) **courage**
yukkuri (adv.) **slowly**
yūmei (adj.) **famous**
yūshoku (n.) **dinner**

zenzen (adv.) **at all (with negative
  verbs)**
zuibun (adv.) **quite, rather**

Index

References in this index are to the Brush-up Section, consisting of the Basics, the Parts of Speech, and the Special Topics, indicated by the symbol § followed by the decimal number.

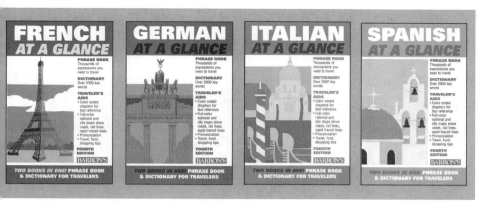

AT A GLANCE Series

Barron's new series gives travelers instant access to the most common idiomatic expressions used during a trip—the kind one needs to know instantly, like "Where can I find a taxi?" and "How much does this cost?"

Organized by situation (arrival, customs, hotel, health, etc.) and containing additional information about pronunciation, grammar, shopping plus special facts about the country, these convenient, pocket-size reference books will be the tourist's most helpful guides.

Special features include a bilingual dictionary section with over 2000 key words, maps of each country and major cities, and helpful phonetic spellings throughout.

Each book paperback, 256 pp., 3 3/4" x 6"

ARABIC AT A GLANCE, 3rd, Wise (978-0-7641-3766-2)
MANDARIN CHINESE AT A GLANCE, 3rd, Seligman & Chen
(978-0-7641-3556-9)
FRENCH AT A GLANCE, 4th, Stein & Wald (978-0-7641-2512-6)
GERMAN AT A GLANCE, 4th, Strutz (978-0-7641-2516-4)
ITALIAN AT A GLANCE, 4th, Costantino (978-0-7641-2513-3)
JAPANESE AT A GLANCE, 4th, Akiyama (978-0-7641-3555-2)
KOREAN AT A GLANCE, Holt (978-0-8120-3998-6)
RUSSIAN AT A GLANCE, Beyer (978-0-7641-3767-9)
SPANISH AT A GLANCE, 4th, Wald (978-0-7641-2514-0)

Barron's Educational Series, Inc.
250 Wireless Blvd., Hauppauge, NY 11788
Call toll-free: 1-800-645-3476
In Canada: Georgetown Book Warehouse, 34 Armstrong Ave.
Georgetown, Ont. L7G 4R9, Call toll-free: 1-800-247-7160

Please visit www.barronseduc.com to view current prices and to order books

(#25) R 7/08

3 Foreign Language Series From Barron's!

The **VERB SERIES** offers more than 300 of the most frequently used verbs.
The **GRAMMAR SERIES** provides complete coverage of the elements of grammar.
The **VOCABULARY SERIES** offers more than 3500 words and phrases with their foreign language translations. Each book: paperback.

FRENCH GRAMMAR
ISBN: 978-0-7641-1351-2

GERMAN GRAMMAR
ISBN: 978-0-8120-4296-2

ITALIAN GRAMMAR
ISBN: 978-0-7641-2060-2

JAPANESE GRAMMAR
ISBN: 978-0-7641-2061-9

RUSSIAN GRAMMAR
ISBN: 978-0-8120-4902-2

SPANISH GRAMMAR
ISBN: 978-0-7641-1615-5

FRENCH VERBS
ISBN: 978-0-7641-1356-7

GERMAN VERBS
ISBN: 978-0-8120-4310-5

ITALIAN VERBS
ISBN: 978-0-7641-2063-3

SPANISH VERBS
ISBN: 978-0-7641-1357-4

FRENCH VOCABULARY
ISBN: 978-0-7641-1999-6

GERMAN VOCABULARY
ISBN: 978-0-8120-4497-3

ITALIAN VOCABULARY
ISBN: 978-0-7641-2190-6

JAPANESE VOCABULARY
ISBN: 978-0-8120-4743-1

RUSSIAN VOCABULARY
ISBN: 978-0-8120-1554-6

SPANISH VOCABULARY
ISBN: 978-0-7641-1985-9

Barron's Educational Series, Inc.
250 Wireless Blvd., Hauppauge, NY 11788
Call toll-free: 1-800-645-3476

In Canada: Georgetown Book Warehouse
34 Armstrong Ave., Georgetown, Ontario L7G 4R9
Call toll-free: 1-800-247-7160

Please visit **www.barronseduc.com**
to view current prices and to order books

LEARN A NEW LANGUAGE
THE FAST, FUN WAY!

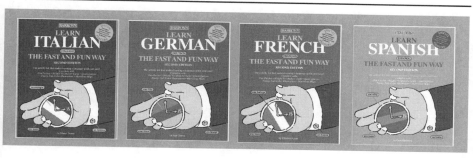

These lively full-color activity books help you pick up the language you need in just minutes a day. Emphasis is on everyday situations—from meeting people and handling simple business transactions to shopping and dining out—and more. All words and phrases are accompanied by pronunciation.

There are hundreds of amusing color illustrations plus puzzles, maps, quizzes and vocabulary cards for practice. *Special bonus for business and vacation travelers:* pull-out bilingual dictionary complete with Food and Drink Guide.

"LEARN A LANGUAGE THE FAST AND FUN WAY" AVAILABLE IN:

ARABIC (ISBN 978-0-7641-4024-2)
CHINESE (ISBN 978-0-8120-9689-7)
LEARN ENGLISH THE FAST AND FUN WAY, 2nd.
(For Russian Speakers) (ISBN 978-0-7641-3623-8)
FRENCH, 3rd Ed. (ISBN 978--0-7641-2559-1)
GERMAN, 3rd Ed. (ISBN 978-0-7641-2540-9)
ITALIAN, 3rd Ed. (ISBN 978-0-7641-2530-0)
JAPANESE, 2nd Ed. (ISBN 978-0-7641-0623-1)
RUSSIAN (ISBN 978-0-8120-4846-9)
SPANISH, 3d Ed. (ISBN 978-0-7641-2550-8)
APRENDA INGLÉS FACIL Y RÁPIDO, 2nd.
(For Spanish Speakers) (ISBN 978-0-7641-0622-4)

Please visit **www.barronseduc.com** to view current prices and to order books

Barron's Educational Series, Inc.
250 Wireless Blvd., Hauppauge, NY 11788

In Canada: Georgetown Book Warehouse
34 Armstrong Ave., Georgetown, Ont. L7G 4R9   (#27) R 7/08